ANTAGONIZING WHITE FEMINISM

Feminist Strategies: Flexible Theories and Resilient Practices

Series Editors: Sharon Labrot Crasnow and Joanne Beil Waugh

Feminist Strategies encourages original work in contemporary philosophical feminism that recognizes that while women have achieved a significant measure of equality, discrimination nonetheless persists through the intersection of gender with other systems and practices of oppression. Such work includes the formulation of theories that are sufficiently flexible, and the promotion of practices sufficiently resilient, to address these changing contexts and forms of oppression. The volumes that comprise this series thus examine current practices, actual cases, and historical episodes of discrimination in which gender has intersected with systems of oppression, including those involving feminism and disability; women, animals, emotion; extended cognition and feminism; women and depression; motherhood; and the new materialist feminism.

Recent titles in the series:

Antagonizing White Feminism: Intersectionality's Critique of Women's Studies and the Academy, edited by Noelle Chaddock and Beth Hinderliter

ANTAGONIZING WHITE FEMINISM

Intersectionality's Critique of Women's Studies and the Academy

Edited by Noelle Chaddock and Beth Hinderliter
Foreword by Beverly Guy-Sheftall

LEXINGTON BOOKS
Lanham • Boulder • New York • London

Published by Lexington Books
An imprint of The Rowman & Littlefield Publishing Group, Inc.
4501 Forbes Boulevard, Suite 200, Lanham, Maryland 20706
www.rowman.com

6 Tinworth Street, London SE11 5AL

Preface epigraph from Patti Duncan's article "Hot Commodities, Cheap Labor: Women of Color in the Academy," *Frontiers: A Journal of Women's Studies* 35, 3 (2014). Reprinted with permission.

British Library Cataloguing in Publication Information Available

Library of Congress Cataloging-in-Publication Data Available

ISBN 9781498588348 (cloth : alk. paper)
ISBN 9781498588362 (paper : alk. paper)
ISBN 9781498588355 (electronic)

The paper used in this publication meets the minimum requirements of American National Standard for Information Sciences Permanence of Paper for Printed Library Materials, ANSI/NISO Z39.48-1992.

CONTENTS

FOREWORD

Beverly Guy-Sheftall

In her recently published anthology, *Are All the Women Still White?: Rethinking Race, Expanding Feminisms*, Janell Hobson reminds us: "The question Are all the women still white? is a loaded inquiry, calling attention to a certain ideology of womanhood and questioning a normalizing and essentializing view of woman that implies a particular race, class, nationality, sexuality, ability, age, and, yes, gender."[1] She also shares that her call for manuscripts for the anthology prompted accusations of an "anti–white women project." Chaddock and Hinderliter's provocative anthology *Antagonizing White Feminism: Intersectionality's Critique of Women's Studies and the Academy* is likely to generate a similar response among readers because of its candid, hard-hitting assessment of women's studies in the academy fifty years after the establishment of the first program at San Diego State University. Its title cleverly suggests a dual meaning—the ways in which mainstream white feminism antagonizes presumably women who are not white and the editors' desire to challenge or antagonize the project of white academic feminism itself. They are confident in their mission: "We have new tools by which to antagonize feminism's exclusionary biases."

This volume is reminiscent of pioneering texts that also "antagonize" white feminisms and the pervasive exclusionary practices of mainstream women's studies, beginning with *All the Women Are White, All the Blacks Are Men, But Some of Us Are Brave: Black Women's Studies.*[2] In particular, this sister collection advocates unapologetically for an "anti-racist, multiplicitous, trans welcoming, different ability accommodating, queer-led, anti-imperialist, decolonial feminism."

Because of my own involvement in the evolution of the development of Women's Studies in the academy, which culminated in my accepting the presidency of the National Women's Studies Association (NWSA) in 2009, I was aware of the field's complex history around difference. My friendship with feminist theorist bell hooks began at the 1981 NWSA conference in Storrs, Connecticut, during which Audre Lorde delivered a ground-breaking, hard-hitting keynote speech, "The Uses of Anger: Women Responding to Racism," in which she spoke about the racism of white women.[3] It was the same year that the Women's Research & Resource Center at Spelman College was founded. Bell was promoting her first book, *Ain't I a Woman: Black Women and Feminism*, at Storrs.[4] We shared a dormitory room, talked all night the first day we met—about the whiteness of the mainstream women's movement and NWSA—and have been talking ever since. In her second book, *Feminist Theory: From Margin to Center*, there is a biting analysis of the insensitivity of Women's Studies to race, class, and ethnicity, and a biting critique of racist writings by white feminists: "White women who dominate feminist discourse, who for the most part make and articulate feminist theory, have little or no understanding of white supremacy as a racial politic, of the psychological impact of class, of their political status within a racist, sexist, capitalist state."[5] Recalling this painful history, I was willing nearly two decades later to join the struggle to help make NWSA an inclusive, multiracial, multicultural, anti-racist organization where women of color and their various feminisms would not be marginalized. We worked hard to center intersectionality in our institutional practices and leadership structure.

Antagonizing white feminism, especially hegemonic cisgender academic feminism, joins a decades-old struggle which many of us assumed would be behind us given the urgency and cogency of anti-imperialist, intersectional, transnational feminist discourse that permeates academic and activist spaces here and around the globe. Ideological and pedagogical challenges to white feminist discourse and exclusionary practices of too many Women's Studies spaces are delineated in a broad range of essays. Despite the truths which this important anthology makes visible, after over fifty years of involvement with

Women's Studies, which began when I was writing a thesis on William Faulkner's treatment of women in his major novels in 1967 at Atlanta University, I am as committed to helping transform this interdisciplinary field as I was when I took my first Women's Studies course as a doctoral student in American Studies at Emory University in 1976. I will include this text in my feminist theory class at Spelman College, the first HBCU with a Women's Studies major, and speak loudly about its value during my annual treks to NWSA conferences. I remain convinced, as do the editors and contributors of this volume, that teaching antiracist, antihomophobic/transphobic, anti-imperialist, intersectional, transnational Women's Studies courses is among the most important work that occurs in the academy. For sure, it is still the most important intellectual work in which I am still engaged.

BIBLIOGRAPHY

Duncan, Patti. "Hot Commodities, Cheap Labor: Women of Color in the Academy." *Frontiers: A Journal of Women's Studies* 35, 3 (2014): 39–63.

Hobson, Janell, ed. *Are All the Women Still White?: Rethinking Race, Expanding Feminisms*. New York: SUNY Press, 2016.

hooks, bell. *Ain't I a Woman: Black Women and Feminism*. 2nd Edition. London: Routledge, 2014.

hooks, bell. *Feminist Theory: From Margin to Center*. 3rd Edition. London: Routledge, 2014.

Hull, Gloria et al. *All the Women Are White, All the Blacks Are Men, But Some of Us Are Brave: Black Women's Studies*. New York: Feminist Press, 1982.

Lorde, Audre. "The Uses of Anger: Women Responding to Racism." (1981) *CUNY Academic Works*.

NOTES

1. Janell Hobson, ed., *Are All the Women Still White?: Rethinking Race, Expanding Feminisms.* (New York: SUNY Press, 2016): 4.
2. Gloria T. Hull, Patricia Bell-Scott and Barbara Smith, eds., *All the Women Are White, All the Blacks Are Men, But Some of Us Are Brave: Black Women's Studies.* (New York: Feminist Press, 1982).
3. Audre Lorde, "The Uses of Anger: Women Responding to Racism." (1981) *CUNY Academic Works.*
4. bell hooks, *Ain't I a Woman: Black Women and Feminism.* 2nd Edition. (London: Routledge, 2014).

5. bell hooks, *Feminist Theory: From Margin to Center.* 3rd Edition. (London: Routledge, 2014): 4.

INTRODUCTION

Antagonizing White Feminism

Noelle Chaddock and Beth Hinderliter

In 2016, many complaints surfaced in feminist discourse in the mass media in the U.S., but also in many global conversations, that white women had "sold out sisterhood." As racial allegiances and securing white privilege and colonial power outstripped the importance of gender equity and liberation for large numbers of white U.S. women in that year's presidential campaigns and election, it became imperative to challenge the systemic failures of feminism and women's[1] spaces with regard to intersectionality. Since 2016 in the United States in particular, but in many instances globally, "women" have organized and advocated for rights in different marches, political protests, online and in their local communities. What became painfully clear in these moments was that the definitions of "women" and "womanhood"—along with who has access to those identities and thus advocacies and membership spaces—was no broader, nor more inclusive (perhaps even less so) than in the 1980s, dominated as they were with the backlash against 1970s activism and the ascendancy of the fundamentalist right-wing "moral majority." This, sadly, is consistent globally.

While locations outside the United States have more visible and diverse organizing in and around resistance to hegemonic and normative constructions of "womanhood," the plight of "the woman" and all things feminine are tied to white, cisgender Western—if not United States—able-bodied, upper-middle-class, educated and able to leverage their academic connections and social capital. For anyone else to participate, they must hyphenate[2] or, at a minimum, precede woman with an adjective. And so, that is where this work starts for us, Chaddock and Hinterliter and our co-conspirators. Most of us are those left in the margins. The rest are those who heard the call to do more than ampersand inclusion. Through cries of #notmyfeminism and "intersectional or bullshit," we have come together to *Antagonize White Feminism.*

We maintain that white feminism remains much the same as it did when white suffragettes excluded women of color in the first wave of feminist activism and organizing in the U.S. and when second-wave feminists likewise excluded the plurality and multiplicity within the voices, concerns and experiences of all women. This was made clear when in 1963 in the United States, Betty Friedan wrote, "The problem lay buried, unspoken, for many years in the minds of American women. It was a strange stirring, a sense of dissatisfaction, a yearning that women suffered in the middle of the twentieth century in the United States. Each suburban wife struggled with it alone."[3] With this, the definition of feminine experiences and womanhood through the twentieth century and into the twenty-first century perpetuated the exclusionary logic of white U.S. suffragettes one century earlier. Despite the many criticisms proffered by women of color collectives, international feminists, womanists, queer feminists, Chicano feminists, trans-feminists, black feminists, womanists and those disavowing feminism altogether from the 1980s to now, this second-wave feminism clung tightly to its structural and systemic endearment towards white, cisgender, heterosexual, hegemonic, academically educated, able-bodied, upper-middle-class identities.

The continued centering of these privileges at the core of feminist discourse and activism might have changed little; however, we have new tools by which to antagonize feminism's exclusionary biases. With our trans kin, we are dismantling biological essentialism and demanding that all of feminism, not just the TERFs (Trans-Exclusionary Radical Feminists), reject the exclusionary biases at the core of who has defined femininity and who has been able to identify as such. With our indigenous families, we are decolonizing settler sexualities and rejecting the Western pathologizing of native bodies, knowledges and practices. We emphasize that sexuality, spirituality and nature are not things to be owned, extracted, or capitalized upon, but sets of relations. Natural forces, bodies of water, or spatial territories are being successfully presented in different courts across the U.S. as Native non-human families and ancestors in need of court protections of their human rights. We are revealing the limitations of our built environments as toxic, poisonous, and regulating and/or restricting of differences between bodies. We are engaging in Afrofuturist world-building that dreams the world we need into being. We are motivated by contemporary practices such as *conjure feminism* that draw on African American hoodoo and herbalist traditions to provide healing and community bonding that resists the trauma and pain of historical and contemporary anti-black racism. These tools are helping us turn the divisions between women that harm and divide us into differences we celebrate as we grow our extended kinship network.

These divisions are not limited to women in the United States, but also are leveraged against women globally as the imperialist occupation of Afghanistan by the U.S. was justified as a war to liberate so-called women of cover. Within the U.S., the 2018 debates during the Supreme Court nomination of Brett Kavanagh revealed how deeply ingrained into society the public shaming of women is, and left many traumatized as they relived their own assaults. Similarly, the November 2018 elections revealed deep divisions between "conservative" or "Trumpian" female voters and who became the deeply conservative and seemingly anti-woman base for the 2018 midterm elections. This tension between women in the United States stands in opposition to the rise of female leaders across the globe.[4]

MARCHING: WHICH WOMEN?

We are deeply troubled by the ways in which some of the most staunch and restrictive membership and authenticity management—that limits claims to *being* a woman or manages whose claims to womanhood count—comes from feminist and Women's Studies spaces that hypocritically claim to offer women solace, advocacy, safety, solidarity, advancement and political salience. One of the things we hope this book will do is help those of us interested in a space where matters impacting woman from birth through any number of lived trajectories figure out how to have a truly intentional, mindful, multiplicitous, solidaritous discourse and praxis—much like what we now call feminism, but better. Vanessa Drew-Branch, Sonyia Richardson, and Laneshia Conner talk about a rebirth of Womanism in their chapter "To Be New, Black, Female and Academic: Renaissance of Womanism within Academia." They are forging the kind of countering work needed to challenge white feminism. But what has been a long-standing concern, most apparent in the organizing of women doing ground-level activist work (protests, lobbying, marches and the like) is the way that white feminism fails not only those it excludes, but also the white, cisgender, upper-middle class women, who are in leadership roles to begin with. Imagine doing hard work and finding out in the end that what your social justice efforts have produced are racist, transphobic, xenophobic, Islamaphobic, anti-Semitic—the opposite of the justice we all claim to be searching for.

From Gloria Steinem's invocation of a populist and monolithic "We, the people" at the Women's March on Washington in January 2017 to Jessa Crispin's *Why I Am Not a Feminist* (2017), which calls for a return to second-wave feminism, mainstream feminism continues to say "we" while invoking only a very narrow population of white, middle- to upper-class, cisgender women. Much of the work of third-wave and international feminists continues to be overlooked. Despite rapidly emerging non-binary and inclusive language available at the intersections of our disciplinary linkages with woman facing feminism, white cisgender feminism continues to ask exceedingly problematic and exclusionary questions such as "Who is a woman"? What are the characteristics of a woman's lived experience? Our work in this anthology aims to disrupt those questions with a few of our own: Who gets to ask such questions? Who will enforce the responses? How can we stretch and flex, if not deconstruct, those characteristics? The voices in this book, and we recognize so many voices are not represented that still have more to contribute to the work, antagonize white cisgender feminism and its self-preservationist fears which have long stood at the heart of the feminist project—that white women will not receive their desired parity with white men if they challenge white supremacist society too radically.

Two moments stand out that led us to the original call for chapter proposals. The first being the attack on Caitlin Jenner and transwomen and the right to self-identify as women no matter how one might perform femininity, from some of the founding voices in second-wave feminism. In the chapter "White Feminism Is the Only Feminism" our author writes about encountering this discourse and understanding its origin from white feminists—they grapple with how one can identify white feminist tropes without knowing the identity of the author. They point us to this reproduction of exclusionary behavior within the transphobic responses of white feminists.

The second moment was the women's marches of 2017, where non-white, non-binary women were reporting exclusion from every aspect of the marches from planning to the language and rhetoric used around them. They talk about the pushback from white feminist organizers when women of color and transwomen raised their concerns. The general response that "the marches are about women's issues only" has plagued feminism since the second wave. Here too, we can see evidence of the enforcement of strict normative ideologies around physical, biological and lived experiences required to call oneself a woman and thus move in feminist space as a woman.

WHITE FEMINISM'S IMPACT OF EXCLUSION IN HIGHER EDUCATION

Despite demands within higher education, specifically within queer studies and student affairs programs, to become more inclusive, we continue to encounter essays and scholarship that throw up walls and barricades around the idea of what it means to be a "woman" from spaces that are often looked at as providing expertise on gender identity and femininity, more specifically. Recent criticism by transnational, African American, Latinx, mixed-race, Indigenous, intersectional, disability and transgender feminists has pointed to an ongoing policing of the feminine within feminist discursive and activist spaces by white feminists, especially within Women's Studies departments and programs in higher education in the West—but most prominently in the United States. While these programs have increasingly changed their names to reflect the spectrum of identities revealed through the concept of gender as opposed to sex or orientation, this has not happened without heated argumentation that women are still oppressed and thus must have women-only spaces maintained. Clearly, women are still oppressed globally. But the intersections at which women live their lives matter. The silencing of those intersections enable white cis-gender feminists to center their marginalization as women—only until non-white non-cisgender feminists enter the space. What, then, is a white feminist in that space, but the dominant privileged person? Left unchecked, she performs that privilege.

In higher education, Women's Studies departments are often some of the most exclusionary spaces, even as they claim to advocate for equity and inclusion; many nonetheless work against gender-inclusive bathrooms, locker rooms, sports teams, affinity groups and other places where those in non-binary and/or fluid positions might expect inclusion. As transwomen, gender variant, and non-gendered scholars emerge, the idea of women and the feminine is unfolding as a suppressive idealism. This exclusionary process seeks to keep feminist or Women's Studies space "women-focused" by disallowing participation or investment in intersectional possibilities like Latinx American Month, for which programing and events are often left to race-based organizations and affiliations with a nod to only doing Women's History Month. We should also note that programming about Latinx women's experiences, left to the Latinx American Studies Program or Committee, is usually far less funded and without access to other resources like dedicated faculty lines and staff. This also often leads to this practice of the non-white interest seeking money and support from the dominant, more established Women's Studies departments in ways that are clearly problematic. Another damaging example—more immediate in its traumatic effects—is sexual assault and violence prevention and survivor care programs that are not inclusive of non-binary, same sex, and transgender relationship violence. As survivors get prescriptively coded as women, often white women exclusively, those who fall outside these boundaries receive different care, or no care at all.

Much feminist focus has been on separating the spheres of sex and gender (similar to earlier separations of race and gender, nationality and gender, immigration and gender), producing a rigidity and exclusionary bias in women's studies that results in exclusion of diverse experiences of the feminine. The recent demands for authentication around womanhood that is tied to trans and homophobic exclusionary ideas of biological sex have gotten to the point of lists of lived experiences that qualify as proof of said "womanhood." The outright dismissal of the concept of the feminine as part and parcel of patriarchal domination has silenced many who may lead with a feminine voice or advance feminine expressions. For example, feminists such as Mary Daly and Germaine Greer dismissed feminine women as "feminine parasites" or "painted birds" and attacked transgender women as fraudulent. The idea that gender (and not sex) is constructed has led to the shaming of transsexuals [*sic*] as not real men or women—and the stigmatizing exclusion of transwomen and their experiences of femininity. Furthermore, the binarism of sex and gender that gets taught in foundational texts in Women's Studies classes (Ortner, Fausto-Sterling) has contributed to a vision of queer liberation as simply sexual or gendered, leading to a right-wing flank of outspokenly racist and gay commentators that repudiate intersectional forms of oppression in order to align with white supremacy and patriarchal forms of privilege. Feminism has been aligned with whiteness as a system of persecution since its inception, and these allegiances must be unlearned so that new forms of radical freedom can be established.

THE FEMININE REFRAMED

The dismissal of the concept of the feminine as false has also allowed the unmarked sphere of masculinity to be continuously advanced as a default setting of identity and experience. Not only has the stigmatization of the feminine as ideological fraud lead to the stigmatization of transgender folk at the hands of feminists, but also has facilitated a new fury within feminism at a younger generation who purportedly claim to wear high heels "just for me" and worry over if waxing means they can't be feminists. Books such as *We Were Once Feminists* (Andy Zeisler) and *Why I Am Not a Feminist* (Jessa Crispin) deride the false consciousness of the feminine as an advertising gimmick for patriarchy, without questioning or engaging the histories of whose femininity is marketed as valuable and whose is discounted. Both authors push back against what they see as the "you go girl" variety of corporate feminism, aiming to return to what they see as the radical feminism or idealist feminism of the 1970s. They advocate disengaging from feminism (not in earnest, though!) despite years of demanding that women who believed in the equality of the sexes had a responsibility to call themselves feminists.

Their dismissal of feminism is not really that; it is more a tongue-in-cheek chastising of feminism's wayward years and a nostalgia campaign for the feminisms of the 1970s. Both chastise notions of a "universal" feminism and the idea of empowerment. "I have a bad case of empowerment fatigue," Andi Zeisler notes in *We Were Feminists Once*. Despite the concept's origins in third-wave feminist challenges to charity-focused, top-down, neo-liberal models of development, empowerment, like feminism itself, Zeisler argues, has now become appropriated and defanged by corporate culture. "Both have become diluted," she writes, "because of the fears about what their definitions stood to change, and in part by the market that's embraced (some) of their goals."[5] Perhaps this is all the more stringent a critique coming from Zeisler, who has long written about the necessity of feminism to engage popular culture. Now demanding a post-marketplace feminism, Zeisler's reimagined feminism feels far afield from the "expansive demands" of third-wave feminism. There is little finesse here between the difference between real empowerment in terms of access to equity in healthcare, education, employment, housing, etc. and gaining buying power within corporate capitalism. Similarly, Jessa Crispin, who is also dismissive of empowerment in *Why I am not a Feminist*, comments that "the idea that you can make the strongest impact by influencing the culture from the inside is naïve at best, disingenuous at worst."[6] Despite admissions that her need for women to identify with feminism was a "shortsighted, non-intersectional perspective," Zeisler still carries forward much of the same exclusionary rhetoric she aimed to criticize. The so-called resurgence of feminist activism has not unlearned much of its biases. And this self-proclaimed ownership over the space by those who identify themselves as "women" or "feminists" has created a hostile, antagonistic relationship for those whose identity expressions and lived experiences do not align with these increasingly unvetted definitions.

As trans identities are increasingly more visible in higher education, those who have spent time in the discourses of the feminine, femininity, feminism, gender, and gender identity are now faced with the realities of reframing those spaces where these identities are considered and ultimately included or excluded. The auto-ethnographic relations of the impact of those spaces, and whether they are thoughtful, intentional, and inclusive, suggest that spaces like "women's studies," "gender and sexuality studies," and "feminism" are not inherently inclusive. This book uncovers and extracts the ways in which feminism and women's studies programs cloak exclusivity in the name of affinity and a history of oppression.

As the national discourse expands to consider, if not critique, what a woman is and whether woman-space-ness should be retained or become inclusive of the diversity of gender identities connected to or intersecting with woman-ness, this book problematizes the singularity and mono-dimensionality through which these discourses are funneled. We would like to have this project serve to call attention to the exclusive, if not hateful, scholarship and discourse coming out of these women-centered spaces and stress that the intersection with the exclusion of trans identities occur consistently across class, race, nationality, and other kinds of difference. The voices within this book create a discourse that is rich with the texture of the feminine in whatever lived experience one might express it through. Our scholar-collaborators in this anthology offer example after example of the narrowness of these proscriptions as they challenge us to deeply consider why and to what end are these exclusions being performed.

"White Feminism Is the only Feminism" challenges feminism as a space for "all" women. They argue that feminism continues to be a constructed and intentional space for white Western, heteronormative, cisgender, able-bodied, academy-related, upper-middle-class women to the exclusion of, and othering of, anyone else. The sense that feminism is an organic space is one of the fictions generated to preserve the space for white, cisgender, middle-class women. The invocation of organic being and product is an attempt to discourage the realities of privilege in that space, allowing white women, specifically, to continue to derive social capital from and speak to their marginalized position. This is a deflective naming of a hegemonic binary space—as counter to the white male, cisgender, heteronormative, able-bodied, academy-related, upper-middle-class space that includes and controls the academe. Chaddock critiques feminist space as an insidiously racist and transphobic space that has far-reaching impacts on the creation of discriminatory spaces across the academy and all industries it informs by leveraging "white women's oppression and marginality" as a foundation for the entitlements of an exclusionary space. Chaddock tells us that not only is she not a feminist, she is not even a woman.

In "Unsettling Dominant Femininities: Promissory Notes Toward an Antiracist Feminist College," Piya Chatterjee asks us to consider the relationship of dominant femininity to "feminism." As she explores the relationships between white American elitism and caste supremacies within India, she demands an unsettling of such elitism nationally, transnationally, and globally. She compels us to recall that in our spaces of higher education even noble aspirations are steeped in cruelty. But what would a transnational, feminist college look like outside of dominant, genteel forms of white cisgender womanhood? The beauty of her promissory note for a future we want to live in is that she asks us to imagine power otherwise in the here and now.

Timothy W. Gerken in his chapter "Repo Fem" offers a performative analysis of both the tyrannies and microaggressions that a gay man faces in leading with a femme voice or identity. By removing the "me" from femme, he repossesses a "fem" identity apart from the bullies and naysayers who "sit in congestion around an identity myth." Struggling against stereotypes and dominant mythologies of the femme gay male, he dismantles these presuppositions about identity. "The Fem's wardrobe, though stylish, cannot be described by any critic: the outfit is designed as it is worn and it is inside out." "Even to each other, fems have difficulty expressing what fem is." So, the troubles unfold: "the fem is not feminism, nor feminist, nor even feminine, but it leads them all both as a prefix and a way of understanding the root and the movement."

Sara Salem engages intersectionality theory as a framework for understanding the dominance of some social categories over others at given moments in time, as she argues in her chapter "White Innocence as a Feminist Discourse: Intersectionality, Trump, and Performances of 'Shock' in Contemporary Politics." She contextualizes the affirmation of Donald Trump by 53 percent of voting white women in the 2016 presidential election in relationship to both the guilt associated with voting for Trump by some, and on the other hand, the innocence on the part of feminists who did not believe it possible that so many white women would vote for Trump. Intersectionality, she argues, pushes feminist scholars to ask what has been left out of the stories we tell, which experiences are valued, and what types of solutions exist to the continuing problems faced by marginalized groups globally and within academia. Intersectionality can also explain the resulting shock on the part of white feminists at the 53 percent statistic, as it suggests the dominance of race, for if there was more attention to the intersections of race, gender, and nation in American society, perhaps shock would not have been the dominant response. Black feminists as well as feminists in the Global South often responded with anger and disappointment, but not shock.

In "Building Kinfulness," Beth Hinderliter argues that white fragility is a major obstacle to building the kinship needed for solidaritous, coalitional politics. Often, solidarity is posed as a precursor to, rather than the effect of, movement work, leading to disappointments, fractured alliances, and failed opportunities for education or change. Asking how can white accountability be taught and/or performed in the classroom, she calls for classroom spaces to be braver and for white women to re-envision what transformative solidarity looks like.

The sixth chapter by Pablo Scharagrodsky and Magalí Pérez Riedel offers an international perspective on the experience of trans women in Argentina. In "Educational Trajectories of the Female Trans Students of the Mocha Celis Secondary School in Argentina," they share the voices and experiences of transgender students at an innovatory school just for transgender youth—the first of its kind in Argentina. As trans women in Argentina have life expectancies of less than forty years, there is an urgent need to understand and overcome the forms of discriminations they face. As the authors make clear, spaces like the Mocha Celis school must navigate the educational and social precarity of transgender youth while countering the discrimination that they face from their peers, family members and society at large.

Vanessa Drew-Branch, Sonyia Richardson, and Laneshia Conner call for a renaissance of Womanism within academia through the telling of the experiences of women of color within higher education who have found the construction of *the feminine* in the traditional sense does not account for their lived experiences of race, gender, and newfound professional identity. In "To Be New, Black, Female, and Academic: Renaissance of Womanism within Academia," they detail how an individual's unique qualities can be perceived as positive or serve as a vulnerability, depending on differing backgrounds and identities. By highlighting the challenges and exclusionary practices that these women face, this chapter shares often overlooked insights that can reframe and reshape the discipline of women's studies.

In "A Rejection of White Feminist Cisgender Allyship: Centering Intersectionality," Beth Hinderliter and Noelle Chaddock offer a cross-racial conversation that theorizes allyship as a detriment to, rather than a bridge towards, a multiracial, multicultural, queer-led, differently abled, anti-imperialist feminism. Theorizing the concept of the "ally-subject," they argue that allies rely on, require even, the continued oppression of their ally-subject. Allies put themselves in the spotlight, are self-congratulatory, and even self-named in their roles. If intersectionality was initially launched as a mode of resistance to mainstream feminism's exclusionary practices, it is often now neutralized by a rhetoric of diversity that invokes, but does not enact, intersectionalism. White Feminism and cisgender women's studies can do more than "engage" such movements as Black Lives Matter as allies: they can locate themselves as co-conspirators. This criticism of allyship is predicated on an understanding that co-conspiracy is a space of shared consequences and a willing loss of social, financial and human capital alongside white cisgender privilege.

BIBLIOGRAPHY

Belangér, Emmanuelle and Verkuyten, Maykel, J. A. M. "Hyphenated Identities and Acculturation: Second Generation Chinese of Canada and the Netherlands." *Identity: An International Journal of Theory and Research, 10*, no. 3 (2010): 141–63.

Crispin, Jessa. *Why I Am Not a Feminist: A Feminist Manifesto*. Melville House, 2017.

Friedan, Betty. *The Feminine Mystique*. Norton and Co., 2001.

Gay, Roxane. *Bad Feminist*. Harper Collins, 2014.

Geiger, Abigail and Kent, Lauren. "Number of Women Leaders Around the World Has Grown But They're Still a Small Group." Retrieved from http://www.pewresearch.org/fact-tank/2017/03/08/women-leaders-around-the-world/. 2018.

Guy-Sheftall, Ed. *Words of Fire: An Anthology of African-American Feminist Thought*. The New Press, 1995.

Hill Collins, Patricia. *Black Feminist Thought: Knowledge, Consciousness, and the Politics of Empowerment*. Routledge, 2002.

hooks, bell. *Feminism Is for Everybody: Passionate Politics*. Second Edition. Routledge, 2014.

Zeisler, Andi. *We Were Feminists Once: From Riot Grrl to CoverGirl™, the Buying and Selling of a Political Movement*. Perseus, 2016

NOTES

1. Chaddock's and Hinderliter's use of *women* and *feminine* outside of direct quotes and paraphrase are inclusive of all female-identified individuals or groups who feel this is an identity at the level of individual identity, political identity, cultural identity, social identity, familial identity or intimate identity. We firmly believe it is not for us to dictate the inclusion or exclusion membership politics of this space.

2. E. Belangér and M. J. A. M. Verkuyten, "Hyphenated Identities and Acculturation: Second Generation Chinese of Canada and the Netherlands." *Identity: An International Journal of Theory and Research, 10* no. 3 (2010): 141–63.

3. Betty Friedan, *The Feminine Mystique*. (New York: W. W. Norton and Co., 2001): 57.

4. According to a 2017 study conducted by the World Economic Forum, the global number of female leaders has more than doubled since 2000. At the time of the study, there were fifteen female world leaders in office, eight of whom were their country's first woman in power. Nonetheless, female leaders still represent less than 10 percent of the 193 UN member states. Abigail Geiger and Lauren Kent, "Number of Women Leaders Around the World Has Grown But They're Still a Small Group," http://www.pewresearch.org/fact-tank/2017/03/08/women-leaders-around-the-world/, accessed November 17, 2018.

5. Andi Zeisler, *We Were Feminists Once: From Riot Grrl to CoverGirl™, the Buying and Selling of a Political Movement*. (New York: Perseus, 2016): 192.

6. Jessa Crispin, *Why I Am Not a Feminist: A Feminist Manifesto*. (Brooklyn, NY: Melville House, 2017): 62.

I

WHITE FEMINISM IS THE ONLY FEMINISM

Noelle Chaddock

During the election contest of 2016, we saw the rise of a group on Facebook that self-identified as the "Pantsuit Nation." When, and for whom, has wearing pantsuits become novel, I wondered to myself? Having been a career-long pantsuit wearer, I didn't get it. I was, however, very aware of the racial demographic of the majority of the newly proclaimed pantsuit wearers. I tried to stay silent, yet as this group gained mainstream traction as a feminist manifestation, I felt marginalized yet again because of my intersectional performances of gender and race. Feminism, especially the forms of feminism which dominate national media outlets, is a particularly cisgender, white, able-bodied, Western/United States–centered, academy-related, upper-middle-class feminism.[1] Despite decades of criticism about the lack of intersectionality of race, gender performance, gender identity, sexual and intimate orientations and class/socio-economic concerns within this white feminism, we see the same exclusionary thoughts and behaviors reproduced and defended. As a colleague, Dr. Reese C. Kelly, has wondered, "Why is the feminism of these individuals really that fragile?" I now find myself wondering if this particular kind of feminism, white feminism, is not only fragile but also implicit in the hegemonic dominance wielded by cisgender, white, able-bodied, Western/United States–centered, academy-related, upper-middle-class women[2] by and through the oppression of women who occupy the intersections, nay, marginal if not opposing positions, to white feminism.

I sadly watched this exclusionary relational violence between white feminism and non-white, non-cisgender, female-identified women unfold during two distinct moments during the election, shaping how we as a nation identify femininity and relate to each other as "women." On December 21, 2016, *The New York Times* published an article[3] about Libby Chamberlain, the creator of the "Pantsuit Nation," which was at that time a nascent Facebook community. The article claimed that Chamberlain had signed a book deal, which was being lauded as a "collective victory" for the Facebook community. Chamberlain is quoted as saying, "A book of YOU. A book BY You," while the article suggests that the only one that will profit from the publication is Chamberlain alone. More importantly, this was not the first division in the Pantsuit Nation community. Several threads were muted or taken down from the original Facebook page because of the tension between white feminist members and women of color. Heidi Stevens penned an article in the *Portland Press Herald* in which Chamberlain and the Pantsuit Nation Facebook community members are said to have "a (mostly) unified space in a bitterly divisive time." Stevens goes on to say that the community "has taken some heat for being self-important and tone deaf—'a space for white people to pat each other on the head for acting in a manner most woke.'"[4] Stevens refers to Erin Gloria Ryan's article in *The Daily Beast*, which takes an even more critical stance against the Pantsuit Nation. Ryan speaks to the thinness of the Pantsuit Nation as a "feminist" institution, which points to, for me, the reality that Chamberlain and company took ownership—and potentially the control of membership authentication—of feminism in a particularly problematic way. The assumptions wrapped up in the role of "the pantsuit" and who does and doesn't wear pants every day is an embodiment of the issue of who get to own feminism. Who gets to name something feminist? Ryan also points to the displays of self-congratulatory whiteness that, in my framing of and experiences with white feminism, plagues white feminist spaces. Ryan says, "What it's devolved into is a space for white people to pat each other on the head for acting in a manner most woke. Some women of color in the group have noted their discomfort with this, only to be ignored or shouted down for interfering with the humming positivity machine."[5]

The second moment that was of particular interest to me coming out of the Trump election in 2016 and the midterm elections of 2018 is the role that white women[6] played in electing a particularly anti-woman and certainly anti-feminist president, administration and officials across the country. Many suggest that white women were and continue to be willing to vote against their and their daughters' self-interest to serve the racist and xenophobic ends of the Trump administration. I went home early from the election party, took a sleep aid, and went to sleep. I knew that there was little I could do, and one more night of sleep would serve me better than the opportunity to co-ruminate. I awoke to an unmeasureable level of communal despondence and despair. The weeping was unexpected and abundant. I had a big job to do in comforting the students at my institution. I shared a single tweet before I headed into what turned into two weeks of service to others. The tweet said "I share your despair, but I cannot share your surprise." I did not shed a tear.

After the 2016 presidential election, for two weeks, there was a line out of my office door of people weeping on my shoulder. Their pain was so real and deep. Folks were traumatized and damaged. In the moment and with critical hindsight, what I came to appreciate was that the most deeply impacted did not seem to be our DACA students, nor our Muslim or Jewish students, it was my white feminist, mostly female-identified, colleagues. They felt betrayed—betrayed by other white women. For myself and other women of color, we were not surprised in any way. White feminists and white women have been doing this kind of sleight of hand for as long as we have been engaging woman-ness, feminism, reproductive and social justice. For me, this was simply the realization of what I as an individual experience regularly. I am no longer vulnerable to this betrayal. What was a surprise, something I am still processing, is the level of fragility demonstrated during that time. I also was deeply aware of the way that I was put into a space of "service to" and not "grieving with." I started tweeting angrily about "self-care" as my self-identified white feminists took more and more time to weep and wallow and the work fell to me and my other colleagues of color. At no point did anyone ask if we might need time for "self-care" or simply to rest from the emotional labor we were doing on top of our regular jobs. After the 2018 midterm elections, the duration of the grieving was not as impactful, but the surprise and upset were still very real. I found myself asking all too often, "Why are you surprised?"

Why do I call out white feminists in such a direct and narrow way? Because every single encounter held a moment where the person I was in service to said, "I am a feminist." It was an ownership. It was not an identity they were attempting to share with me. It was a badge of honor. It was a conflation of individual positionality and universal framework. It was an invocation of unexamined privilege. I hope that our examination of feminism, white feminism, allows for a deconstruction of feminism and an examination of how feminism has managed, wave after wave, to remain white (despite the proximity of women of color) and intentionally cisgender (against the public requests from transwomen for inclusion). Finally, I had a moment where I had to say out loud, "If you are crying on a person of color's shoulder, allowing them to comfort you, please take a moment to think about whether you are reciprocating. If you are not, they are in service to you." And this is my problem.

The pronouncement of majority identity packaged as self-realization, or as Ryan positions it as "acting in a manner most woke," must be challenged. It is not enough, as was proven in the 2016 presidential election and again in the 2018 midterm elections, to say one is a feminist. It is not enough to publically own one's whiteness, straightness, or cisgenderness without being willing to alter the path of those who are negatively impacted by those identities. Instead of crying or organizing national marches for women where exclusionary violence goes unchecked, white feminists could be thinking more deeply about their contributions to the problem. What does it mean to be a white feminist? Does the invocation of such require immediate appreciation and welcoming from those marginalized in the white feminist space? How many waves of feminism will it take before we have a theoretical and praxical feminism that includes "black feminism" "transfeminism," "international feminism," etc.? I had a moment of hope around the "Women's March on Washington" as it rolled out in cities across the nation, especially in my own city of Memphis, Tennessee, which is a 60+ percent black city. That hope faded almost immediately when my hyper-focused googling of organizers suggested a lack of race, class, ability, nationality and gender identity. The remote event pictures and social media posts and exchanges supported my suspicion that yet again intersectionality and diversity were secondary thoughts in the planning of an "all" women's march. Again, Facebook and Twitter erupted with complaints from transwomen and women of color about the lack of organic inclusion. And, again, white feminists reclaimed "the movement" for themselves with their fragility, claims of victimization as a result of this criticism, and tears—lots of tears. All of this reoccurred around the November 2018 midterm elections which followed the contentious appointment of Brett Kavanaugh to the Supreme Court despite a sexual assault claim made against him. More women's marches were organized which, again, lacked the diversity one would have anticipated understanding the need for a solidaritous voting strategy. Marches entitled "women's marches" were majority white, while white feminist allies were woefully underrepresented at the Black Women's March in October 2018. White women voted again, not the majority but close, seemingly against their own civil rights. Up to the night of actual voting, what has now come to be known as black Twitter and Facebook were alive with the question "What will white women do?"

I no longer claim feminism as a core identity, not as a person nor a scholar. I haven't found great replacement language for my human and scholarly focus around those who identify as "woman," but I know that a feminism by and for white, cisgender, able-bodied, Western/United States–centered, academy-related, upper-middle-class women is not what I am interested in doing or being part of. This has been a long scholarly and intellectual struggle for me. I have a graduate certificate in feminism but cannot get a job in my discipline. I can only teach in Africana Studies, which I love, but that is not what I trained for. My narrative of exclusion from the white feminist space and my re-exclusion from the "feminine" space is real, pervasive and painful. As a critical race scholar, as a black woman of color, as a daughter of a white adoptive mother, I struggle to understand the lack of consciousness and the level of fragility demonstrated by white feminism. I usually do critical work around systems and systemic conditions, but this is personal, and I intersect with this more deeply than any other identity. I have lost friends. I have walked away from collegial collaborators because I just cannot carry the load any longer. It has been an exhausting journey. I have disavowed ideas of self-care for the necessary work of self-healing.

Upon arriving at my first institution after graduate school, I sought out my sister feminists in the Women's Studies program. I then understood myself as a feminist, had a graduate certificate in feminism, and was eager to be part of the Women's Studies program. I was received with an articulation of hesitation. There was a concern from the program director about making sure the content of my courses met a certain standard or quality of other courses offered to their majors. That seemed reasonable, and I was certain I could meet that standard. My proposals for courses were not rejected, they were simply ignored. In ten years with that institution, I did not teach a single course in the Women's Studies program despite the lack of course offerings and faculty. During the advent of the first "Women's History Month" at the college, I tracked down the program director who was organizing programming for the month. I proposed my talk "On Being a Black Woman." I was told, in a particularly patronizing way, that my talk would have been better suited for last semester . . . Black History Month.

During my time as a diversity officer in my early career, I worked to move my campus community towards holistic institutional gender inclusion. One of my colleagues, a self-identified feminist, was working with me in several areas around gender inclusion. We shared articles and had conversations almost daily. During a meeting with athletics staff, we had an opportunity to talk about gendered sports teams on our campus and the challenges of National Collegiate Athletic Association (NCAA) rules around transathletes. Our athletics department was looking to create a trans-inclusive policy for athletes. In the meeting, we started to get pushback around gender-inclusive teams. I suggested we offer gender inclusivity, rather than trans inclusivity, allowing us to be more fluid with our ability to provide equitable and inclusive spaces for athletes. The athletics staff was immoveable around binary gender and the need for space for "each gender," and there was no middle ground except co-ed (already gender inclusive, by the way) teams, which were few. I looked to my sister feminists in a moment of what I thought was solidarity, to which they said, "I think we need to preserve the spaces for women that we have fought so hard for since we are still not fully equal." "What if men decide to take over women's teams?" I don't have a clear recollection of what was said after that. My ears were ringing. My brain and heart shut down. What I heard in that moment was that it was acceptable to this daily Facebook-posting feminist that anyone who could not claim cisgender women-ness would be excluded in our feminism and in our inclusion efforts. After the meeting, I reached out to better understand my colleague's position. In that conversation, they reaffirmed that they did not think there should be a "dilution" of "female" spaces.

Around the same time as the gender-inclusive team failure, our Women's Studies program committee members were grappling with a name change proposal. The proposal was from one of the professors that educated me in my graduate school feminist program at a different institution and whom I was so excited to have join us at this institution because I was certain that they would bring frameworks to problematize what I was experiencing in the current space I was trying to contribute to. My graduate school professor and mentor was proposing a name change to Women's Studies and Sexuality because she taught sexuality studies. Another colleague suggested that this was an opportunity to broaden the program's scope to reflect the need for gender inclusion in this program. The proposal was now Gender and Sexuality Studies. The white feminists on our campus, including my graduate school professor, pushed back with all of their cisgender power and dominance, refusing to give up Women in the title because they were not yet equal to men—cisgender white men—and they had fought hard for a women's space—a cisgender white women's space. Because of the lack of diversity in the space, I was not part of the conversation. The program retained, even with new leadership, their white, cisgender, middle-classed program in name and content.

Finally, the event that caused me to create this discursive space in which we are currently writing and reading was the feminist—white, cisgender, middle-classed—pushback against Caitlyn Jenner. In a *Huffington Post* article from June 6, 2015, Elinor Burkett constructs an atrocious proscription of the rigors of membership into a "feminine" space and a "female" identity.[7] I reached my limit around accepting or ignoring and avoiding this conversation. My reading of Burkett is that they are writing that almost any woman who did not have their particular "feminine" experience was not "real woman." When I first read the article, I was with a colleague of mine, and I said to them, "How do white women keep producing this kind of exclusionary discourse?" and they said, "Wow, Noelle that is really racist. . . . How do you know this author is white?" What a great question. Why do I know that this author is white? Why am I confronted with the author's white dominance and violence? I was so certain that the author's whiteness played a defining role in their position that they had the right and power to rewrite anyone's gender and identity membership. Somehow, I just *knew*. My colleague and I looked up the author. I was right. I was able to identify white feminism without any visual evidence. It was long after we started this book project and I read chapter after chapter from women of color about their exclusion from feminist discourse and spaces that I realized I had recognized the white exclusionary behavior in that article through an experientially informed lens. This author had written the same argument, the exact framing and reframing that excluded me as a woman of color from the white feminist space. This was the final framing of my lived realities and scholarly location as intensely not feminist. I have been written out of the feminist space. I have always understood myself as reframed, as not "feminine," but I had always believed I was articulated as "feminist." I have been rewritten by the very people who claimed to be in sisterhood and solidarity with me and who claimed to be "people like me." I cannot imagine a greater ideological betrayal.

I am not a feminist. I am not a woman. In the discursive and physical spaces of "the feminine," I am re-framed and re-named in ways that are not familiar to me. I am often, if not always, relegated to spaces that are nameless, isolated . . . marginalized. My theories on "woman-ness" push against what is often articulated as "traditional feminism." I am relegated to a hyphenated feminism that is devalued by this "traditional feminist" space—by white feminism. My worth and scholarly, human contributions seem only to exist before the hyphen "black-"and my "feminine" has been suspended. The labor of my blackness is appropriated, stretched, referenced, and taught by my white feminist peers while I am blocked out of those spaces. I am appointed to Africana Studies, never Women's Studies, and my requests to cross list my black feminism is met with a request to change the title and focus my course as "someone else," a white feminist, is already teaching black feminism.

For there to be black feminism, there must be white feminism. For there to be transfeminism, there must be cisgender feminism. Where are our white lesbian feminists who fought to be included in the feminist discourse and the framing of "feminine"? At times, it seems as if white lesbian feminism takes up the tenor of the white cisgender feminist space when there is a performance of exclusion towards transwomen. In my experiences, white lesbian feminists have perpetuated, rather than challenged, the ways that Women's Studies and other advocacy groups should include a T in the LGB work they are doing. The reason for my calling out white lesbians in this chapter, along with white feminists in particular, is to flesh out the power of whiteness as it plays a role in destroying solidaritous spaces. This is about how whiteness seemingly destroys intersectional identities to leave only whiteness. Over the last few years I have seen a shift in the indicators used to signal safe spaces and welcoming colleagues and conversations. White feminists and white lesbians (I was naïve) always signaled safe spaces for me as a person and for my scholarship. Now I experience those spaces as perpetuation of systemic inequities and bias. A space that once invited contentious discourse now shuts down conversations of race and racism as it is performed by, in, and through the white feminist institution. Perhaps that is the conversation, that feminism is now a capitalist hegemonic institution with all the dressings and functions of other such institutions.

When there is an invocation of feminism, or the "we" as feminists, there is an immediate exclusion of women outside of white, cisgender, middle-class identity, in that multiplicitous feminisms are not being engaged, or are intentionally being avoided, in those moments. During the content acquisition provided in my graduate certificate in feminism, if any non-majority feminism was offered, it was named and framed as outside of the feminist cannon; i.e., bell hooks is a black feminist. This sense of white-centric feminism goes unchallenged even by its non-white consumers. Claiming feminism for themselves, for white cisgender feminists, to the end of not referring to their work as white and/or cisgender feminism, is a leveraging of white and cisgender privilege and normativity that must be teased out of the larger conversations of exclusive "feminine" discourses.

The performance of whiteness, gender normativity, white and gender dominance, and white and cisgender privilege that allows white cisgender theorists to claim feminism as their exclusive, privileged space extends beyond the discursive space into the programmatic spaces of academe. Women's Studies programs and departments are maintaining an insidiously racist and transphobic space in universities, where the indoctrination of new white, cisgender feminists goes unnoticed and thus unchallenged. The self-preservationist practices of these spaces, the programming for and about white cisgender women-ness, serves to solidify the dominate positon of white cisgender, white, able-bodied, Western/United States–centered, academy-related, upper-middle-class women in the space then framed as the "feminine" and feminist.

The hegemonic power, privilege and dominance of white feminism become public and overt in the transphobic attacks from Germaine Greer, renowned and iconic feminist, against Caitlyn Jenner in fall 2015. The *New York Post* reported Greer saying, "Just because you lop off your d**k and then wear a dress doesn't make you a f***ing woman. . . . I've asked my doctor to give me long ears and liver spots and I'm going to wear a brown coat but that doesn't turn me into a f***ing cocker spaniel."[8] And the feminist community applauded actress and feminist Rose McGowan's very public "schooling" of Jenner on social media. McGowan railed, "You're a woman now? Well f***ing learn that we have had a VERY different experience than your life of male privilege."[9]

White feminists like Burkett from Pantsuit Nation affirm my own exclusion from the "feminine" and feminist space. Burkett's ability, privilege, right to both define membership to authentic "women-ness" as a required experience of having "woken up after sex terrified they'd forgotten to take their birth control pills the day before . . . had to cope with the onset of their periods in the middle of a crowded subway," while reducing blackness to "using chemicals to change his skin pigmentation and crocheting his hair into twists" in the most racist of analogies to the transgender experience suggests the feminist devaluing of trans and black women in a single moment. When Burkett opines, "Their truth is not my truth. Their female identities are not my female identity." I respond in mighty voice and soul-felt resistance—and yours is not mine. And mine, my truth, my "feminine," my "feminist discourse" is not included. In a single moment, the realities of feminism and the "feminine" as singularly white cisgender spaces is clear. White cisgender feminists appear to feel that they have the right to check membership at the "feminine" door, which is hugely problematic and has reduced the numbers of feminists by many.

I remember a peer in graduate school asking me how any "woman" could not be a feminist. Beyond the obvious problems weaved through this question, I now appreciate that the more important part of this exchange is who is defining "woman" and "woman like me." When white feminists intentionally block intersectional conversation in spaces dedicated to examinations and advocacy for "women" or the "feminine," they are creating an exclusionary space. The only recourse that folks like me have is to leave and/or resist entering those exclusionary spaces. As women of color leave the feminist space (and white women refuse to check in with them over their departures), feminism becomes nearly monolithic and unmitigated in its privilege and hegemonic dominance. I can only speak for myself and colleagues who have shared and helped me articulate this sentiment. We have left because your transphobic rhetoric is a reproduction of the harm we experienced when you excluded us for our race. We remember all of the times we were told not to talk about race because "this meeting is about women's issues not race issues."

I leave you with this. My issues of gender, race, class, ability, and nationality are inseparable. I am now holding you accountable to own your gender, race, class, ability, and nationality in relationship to each other if you are a white feminist. I will forever expect, if not require, if I am to be in relationship or community with you, that you refer to the realities of yourselves as a white feminist. If you and your scholarly spaces can refer to me and others as black or trans feminists, you can no longer just be a feminist.

Lastly, when I do encounter non-white, non-cisgender feminisms being taught by white cisgender feminists, it is in this almost fetishized way. It is important when any of us do feminist work outside our lived experiences, especially if we are privileged in relationship to those experiences, I beg that we resist teaching the other as a sexy, more attractive, and marketable scholarship. Feminism, white feminism, must stop rewriting black and trans women in its discourse, studies, and programming. To allow these kinds of slippages is to allow a writing of the other without permission, without information, without relationship, and, by and large . . . we are doing it wrong.

BIBLIOGRAPHY

Alter, Alexandra. "A Book Deal for Pantsuit Nation and Then a Backlash." *The New York Times*, December 21, 2016. http://www.nytimes.com/2016/12/21/business/a-book-deal-for-pantsuit-nation-and-then-a-backlash.html?_r=0.

Burkett, Elinor. "What Makes a Woman." *The New York Times*, June 6, 2015. http://www.nytimes.com/2015/06/07/opinion/sunday/what-makes-a-woman.html?smid=fb-nytimes&smtyp=cur&_r=2.
Crenshaw, Kimberlé. "Demarginalizing the Intersection of Race and Sex: A Black Feminist Critique of Antidiscrimination Doctrine, Feminist Theory, and Antiracist Politics." *University of Chicago Legal Forum, 8* (1989): 1399–67.
Crenshaw, Kimberlé. *On Intersectionality: Essential Writings*. New York: The New Press, 2019.
Ferber, Taylore. "Rose McGowan Schools Caitlyn Jenner with Much Needed Feminism 101." *VH1 News*, November 17, 2015. http://www.vh1.com/news/224136/rose-mcgowan-shuts-down-caitlyn-jenner-glamour-award/?xrs=_s.fb_vh1main.
Gay, Roxane. *Bad Feminist: Essays*. New York: Harper Perennial, 2014.
Lukas, Carrie. "There's a Feminist War Brewing over Caitlyn Jenner." *The New York Post*, October 26, 2015. http://nypost.com/2015/10/26/theres-a-feminist-civil-war-brewing-over-caitlyn-jenner/.
Ryan, Erin Gloria. "Pantsuit Nation Is the Worst: Why a Book of Uplifting Facebook Posts Won't Heal America." *The Daily Beast*, December 21, 2016. http://www.thedailybeast.com/articles/2016/12/21/pantsuit-nation-is-the-worst-why-a-book-of-uplifting-facebook-posts-won-t-heal-america.html.
Stevens, Helen. "Commentary: Pantsuit Nation Won't Stay in Style without More Inclusion, Less Smugness." *Portland Press Herald*, December 28, 2016. http://www.pressherald.com/2016/12/27/commentary-pantsuit-nation-wont-stay-in-style-without-more-inclusion-less-smug/.

NOTES

1. In this article, "cisgender, white, able-bodied, Western/United States–centered, academy-related, upper-middle-class" will often be represented by the term "white feminism."

2. I use *women* in this essay as inclusive of all female-identified individuals or groups that call themselves women.

3. Alexandra Alter, "A Book Deal for Pantsuit Nation and Then a Backlash." *The New York Times* (December 21, 2016), http://www.nytimes.com/2016/12/21/business/a-book-deal-for-pantsuit-nation-and-then-a-backlash.html?_r=0, accessed on December 11, 2017.

4. Heidi Stevens, "Commentary: Pantsuit Nation Won't Stay in Style without More Inclusion, Less Smugness," *Portland Press Herald* (December 28, 2016), http://www.pressherald.com/2016/12/27/commentary-pantsuit-nation-wont-stay-in-style-without-more-inclusion-less-smug/, accessed on February 12, 2017.

5. Erin Gloria Ryan, "Pantsuit Nation Is the Worst: Why a Book of Uplifting Facebook Posts Won't Heal America," *The Daily Beast* (December 21, 2016), http://www.thedailybeast.com/articles/2016/12/21/pantsuit-nation-is-the-worst-why-a-book-of-uplifting-facebook-posts-won-t-heal-america.html, accessed on January 25, 2017.

6. White women speaks to both those who self-identify as white women and those who are identified by polling software/data collection programs as white women.

7. Elinor Burkett, "What Makes a Woman," *The New York Times*, June 6, 2015, http://www.nytimes.com/2015/06/07/opinion/sunday/what-makes-a-woman.html?smid=fb-nytimes&smtyp=cur&_r=2, accessed on December 8, 2017.

8. Carrie Lukas, "There's a Feminist War Brewing over Caitlyn Jenner," *The New York Post*, October 26, 2015, http://nypost.com/2015/10/26/theres-a-feminist-civil-war-brewing-over-caitlyn-jenner/, accessed on December 8, 2017.

9. Taylore Ferber, "Rose McGowan Schools Caitlyn Jenner with Much Needed Feminism 101," *VH1 News*, November 17, 2015, http://www.vh1.com/news/224136/rose-mcgowan-shuts-down-caitlyn-jenner-glamour-award/?xrs=_s.fb_vh1main, accessed on December 8, 2017.

2

UNSETTLING DOMINANT FEMININITIES

Promissory Notes Toward an Antiracist Feminist College

Piya Chatterjee

I was walking behind a slender white woman wearing jodhpurs and tall riding boots, blonde straight hair slicked into a pony tail. It was sometime in early October 2012.[1] I remember the moment with some vividness because I had just arrived to take up my new appointment as a professor of Gender and Women's Studies at Scripps College after teaching for eighteen years at the University of California-Riverside (UCR). I was still taking it all in, as the ethnographer I am: the particularly beautiful and immaculate grounds of the college and trying to figure out its architecture and spatial layout—Spanish mission-style walls, perfect lawns, and café-like chairs in patio settings. It was also quiet, and the young people I encountered gave me quiet and friendly smiles. Then, suddenly, this vision in jodhpurs—looking like she had just stepped out of *Town and Country* or *Tatler*—walked quickly in front of me. It took me a second to realize that she was wearing riding gear. I realized I had entered a very different world of higher education. It was a jolt, I confess. I experienced that precise moment as if I was falling down the proverbial rabbit hole, albeit more as a foreign brown Alice, into a world that I had glimpsed from afar. I panicked—how was I ever going to translate my particular antiracist and Third

World feminist pedagogies to students who might come from these incredible words of jodhpur-clad privilege? What had possessed me to leave a tenured position at UCR for this new landscape of education?

I reflect back on that question in the seven years that have passed. I have taught some remarkable students at Scripps College and the Claremont Consortium. Many were from highly privileged and elite backgrounds; a few have been first-generation students of color—most have "self-selected" to be in a feminist classroom. I already knew from my years of teaching at UCR that, on the whole, this usually translated into an open-ness and curiosity to being challenged and challenging themselves around questions of power, racisms, patriarchy, and privilege. I was fortunate, then, to be able to have these kinds of pedagogical energies in the classroom, even when resistance to the material was palpable in some instances, especially when I was pushing antiracist intersectional feminist material.

The students and I together have sometimes recognized that the framework of a "women's college" can both constrain and expand our understandings of what learning/teaching gender(s), justice and education in our current historical and political moment might mean. For one, the struggles of co-eval access to education for subjects who are "women," globally, remains a significant one. But as we incorporate transgender, queer, antiracist and explicitly *antiracist* and *anticasteist* intersectional perspectives in our feminist curriculum, we recognize the continued importance of challenging the very terms, and foundations, of gender itself—and that means blowing open the binaries upon which the categories of gender are constructed, and mixing that together with vital analysis of "interlocking and simultaneous oppressions," in the terms of the Combahee River Collective.[2]

The Scripps' classroom, in fact, has been an extraordinarily provocative space within which we have sharpened our scalpels, and understandings, about how we are variously socialized into our gendered subjectivities. What does it mean to be "women"? What is "femininity," and how can we think of this in the plural and through an anti-racist intersectional lens? How does class privilege shape our understanding of "femininity"? What about "masculinity"? What if we don't experience ourselves as either "women" or "men"? How can we expand our definitions beyond binaries and into the plural—masculinities, femininities? What guidelines do transgender feminists offer for us to think about such pluralities of gender within the matrices of racisms and patriarchy?

For the purposes of this chapter, and its preliminary reflections, I will parse out some of the tensions of teasing some of these broad and obvious questions from within the particular landscape of an elite liberal arts women's college. What are the forms of "femininity" that underwrite the production of the "women's college" student? How are these manifested? What is the relationship of this "femininity" to the "feminism" that is institutionally produced or perceived? How does whiteness and/or caste-privilege inform this production? And class? Crucially, how do non-binary, gender nonconforming and transgender experiences push us to revision our ethics of gender justice in this time?

In these promissory notes, I will suggest that there is an urgent need to both excavate, and unsettle, the terms of dominant femininities. I use the verb "unsettle" to precisely gesture to the terms of settler colonialism upon which all these questions and imaginaries need to be based. The beautiful Spanish-style architecture does not only bound the immaculate space of the college—it also signals the violent history of indigenous erasure.

Within the microcosm of a small women's liberal arts college, all of these questions—and the gesture to foundational settler colonialism—might be an ethnographic curiosity, merely academic. However, given the racialized and gendered demographics of the election of an openly misogynistic and anti-feminist president and his administration's regressive policies, it behooves us to think in more nuanced ways about racial and gendered demographic patterns of the vote, but specifically the ideologies of racialized gender that play out in the everyday practices of liberalism—and an elite liberal arts women's college is certainly one site where the fault lines of individual liberalism and mainstream feminism (presumed to be progressive and liberatory) can be masked.

For example, how does a personal, individual sense of feminism and identity ("I am a feminist because I am at a women's college")—woman qua feminist—reconcile with the huge cross-class support that many white women offered to this president by voting for him? When we are working (as teachers and learners) in a predominantly white institution that espouses a particular kind of feminist ethos in its messaging, then the questions of class and racial privilege, in particular, are compelled to take center stage within the national context of open, state-supported policies of white supremacy. This not only pushes the curricular formation and pedagogical experiences within feminist classrooms, it also opens up very critical questions about the history, mission and contemporary praxis of women's colleges.

It is beyond the scope of this short chapter to do full justice to the questions I have posed, and I will not be able to follow through them adequately because they gesture to both important pedagogical questions as well as how these might shift the governance and foundational structures of the antiracist feminist college that I am imagining. I merely offer them as pointers for the provocations that I offer—and the dreams that occasionally flit through my consciousness when I learn and teach with my students and colleagues. I will touch upon the following themes through an auto-ethnographic and autobiographical method that is pulled primarily from memories of classroom discussions. Please view these as "traces"—moments which need to be much more fully fleshed. These are very much promissory notes—a few steps toward radically imagining what an anti-racist feminist college, explicitly defined as such, might look like. That is for a larger project. But for now, the first bits of chiseling away.

REFRACTING DOMINANT FEMININITY I: TRANSNATIONAL CASTE PRIVILEGE

When I momentarily encounter the high-fashion privilege of jodhpurs, I know that I have entered a world of a feminized gentility and privilege that harkens to old British colonial worlds that I have some familiarity with: the riding breeches, jodhpurs, comes from the name of the Indian city of Jodhpur, where polo became the game of both English rulers and their crony-puppet Maharajas. As an Indian immigrant, educated in new empire, I am struck by that irony.

I also reflect on the question ending my introductory paragraph—*what had possessed me?*—and realize that my shift to Scripps had everything to do with my own journey into the U.S. academy and how it was steeped in transnational caste privilege.[3] The geopolitics and histories of such privileged social contours of travel and migration are not accidental. Certainly, I was trying to escape alienating and toxic workplace dynamics at UCR, and I was burned out. When offered this job—advertised for a senior scholar doing work around transnational feminisms and social justice—it sounded like a great fit.

I also knew I was attracted to the position because I had graduated from Wellesley—my first point of entry as a foreign student in the United States in 1983. There was something about teaching at a "women's college" that brought back a certain kind of nostalgia for my own college days. However, this nostalgia did erase the issues of elitism, of whiteness and class privilege, that had also made the Wellesley experience a vexed one for me, a foreign student on almost full scholarship. Still, there was something about Wellesley that I cherished. Digging deeper, I understand several things about Wellesley's impact on my formation as a "feminist." First, as a woman who was only beginning to come to her "own" in a foreign country, I did not question the Wellesley woman-empowerment ideology as one that might be steeped in cisgender privilege, whiteness, class power and empire. The woman/power thing was hugely appealing and seductive, and I embraced it wholly. At that time, it never dawned on me to ask deeper questions about being a "woman," and I did not take one feminist studies course at the college.

Second, I was a young Brahmin-*savarna* woman from an American international boarding school, which was ironically founded as a Protestant missionary school for women in 1854 by the British.[4] I was already well acculturated towards the "west," its cultural norms. Through this boarding-school education which I started at the age of eight, I was already white-adjacent in terms of my sense and entitlement towards upward mobility, and even comfort in terms of who I mixed with—the faculty of my school came from mostly white American or European backgrounds though there were some Indian staff, and most of my Indian peers were themselves from *savarna* and highly elite class backgrounds. The school is incredibly international, so many of my close friends growing up were white European or American—but in those days and especially in India, the term "white" was not used as a descriptor. I grew up relatively unaware of both racial and caste privilege—which is, of course, a direct consequence of that very privilege.

This opportunity was vitally supported by a father who invested in my education and was progressive about women's education. All this material support and encouragement created a smooth road, built on shared social capital, that paved my entry into the world of Wellesley. It meant that I could easily embrace, and also feel psychologically empowered, by explicit institutional messages around ciswomen's leadership at a place like Wellesley. That this was also racially inflected was not something I was fully aware of until much later.

In short, this sense of entitlement to a great education in new empire, cultivated by a fine secondary school from old empire, was structurally enabled by caste and class power. I was primed to accept the messages of excellence and exceptionalism. Wellesley has a storied history of supporting international students (including most famously, Princess May Ling Soong/Madame Chiang Kai Shek) and offering need-blind financial aid (which is how I made it), and we were nurtured and welcomed in many ways. I will never forget the first orientation meeting at Slater International House where a distinguished alumna, the first African American woman on the Board of Trustees of Harvard Business School, exhorted us to become leaders. "Introduce yourselves to the person to your right," she said, "who knows, you might be shaking the hands of a future president." Enabled by caste and class privilege, my own sense of emerging womanhood—and femininity—meshed with the entitled feminized leadership/empowerment narrative presented by the college, I never questioned the messaging until much later. Polished, highly educated, cosmopolitan, cisgender white or white-adjacent women could, indeed, run the world. Hillary Clintons, of all hues, step up.

REFRACTING DOMINANT FEMININITY 2: LANDSCAPES, SILENCES, BODIES

In making a choice to leave a tenured UC job, I had "forgotten" the codes of privilege and power that constituted the warp and weft of a place like Wellesley. It has been jarring to admit that this "forgetting" was actually part of a subconscious normalizing—an acceptance and even desire for bourgeois white and white-adjacent femininity that was sharply mediated by my caste and class privilege. Yet, eighteen years of teaching at UCR had also made me profoundly aware of the ground realities of gender, class, and U.S. racial politics in higher education.

UCR students had forever transformed my understanding of social capital and education, my own journey as a privileged immigrant, and perhaps America itself.

I have written elsewhere about the particular challenges of those public university classrooms and what they taught me about the pedagogies of the possible. I knew, leaving UCR for Scripps, that what I would regret most was leaving the UCR classroom—the incredible ethno-racial and class diversities that has made the university such a unique institution, even in the UC system. So, I came to Scripps as a teacher who had been tested about her privilege by the very composition of the UCR classroom, and whose understanding of entitlement and privilege had shifted quite radically. I was no longer comfortable with being "white adjacent" and taught more confidently as a "woman of color."

The pedagogical challenge in this new landscape was how I was going to persuade my students to hone in on their own privileges and what Adrienne Rich has called "a politics of location." I started to tackle this directly by privileging U.S. women-of-color critiques of white supremacy and then offering distinct modules around the construction of white womanhood, historically and in the contemporary period. I assigned readings by antiracist white feminists (like Minne Bruce Pratt or Ruth Frankenberg) and compelled all students to think about whiteness and femininity in explicit ways—as a historical construction, and particular to regions and places. In these classes, self-identified white students and students of color brought up their questions about the women's college project, and particularly Scripps itself. We also talked about plantation histories, constructions of white chastity, the complicities of white women's violence in plantation patriarchies. Several students started their own antiracist discussions as self-identified white students and set up their own Facebook page.

Through this pedagogical work, I also started thinking of the analogues of caste and white supremacy and the ways in which my own subjectivity, as a Brahmin-*savarna* woman—was implicated in supremacist logics. I began to read, and assign, Dalit, Muslim and Adivasi gender justice writers as a way to begin to think about my own complicities with supremacist and feminized logics, and also make the important transnational connections between whiteness and caste power. There is much more to say here, and I gesture to this not lightly—or as a move to some form of caste-innocence.[5]

Rather, it is to assert that the sustained focus on antiracist feminist work on white womanhood, and the relationship of whiteness to the construction of dominant femininity, compelled me to re-think and read anew some of the brilliant, incisive work forwarded by Dalit feminists, in particular, about casteist feminisms and dominant femininities in South Asia. It has also asked me to push much further into the resonances—and indeed the dovetailing—of both white and caste supremacies in the formation of dominant femininities. The "unsettling" is a project that is national, transnational, global.

In the classroom, we discussed how mainstream student culture at Scripps upheld whiteness through both its landscapes, its temporalities, and the kind of feminized bodies that moved through its spaces. Strikingly, students themselves suggested how Scripps women fit into the idealized norms of dominant beauty norms: thin, white, expensive fashion aesthetics, a particular kind of "cloned" look of active, cisgender, pretty bodies. In my classes, students have talked about eating disorders and how prevalent this was in the college and how the dominant norm was deeply unhealthy, and not addressed openly. Some students have done excellent (thesis) projects on fatphobia and body positivity, linking racism and constructions of femininity in brilliant ways. Even then, these critiques have happened on the edges of the institution, a mindful cultivation of margins *a la* bell hooks.

Our discussions also shifted our attention sometimes to the architectural and spatial arrangements of the college. A small campus, Scripps has exquisite grounds—its California mission style includes adobe walls that surround the campus, tiles, and some beautiful courtyards. It does not escape us (as I noted earlier) that this beauty explicitly mimics the vernacular styles of Spanish settler colonialism. The walls surround almost the entire campus, convent-like. Here, it seems, young girls and women might be cocooned in a kind of immaculate quiet—and emerge with an education in creative virtue. For many of us who come from cultures of dense and lively sociality, this empty space and the silence it contains can feel alienating and repressive.

In some of our discussions, a few students talk about how they love the silence, quiet, and peace. But others—usually not white—speak of a silence that makes them uncomfortable. It is particularly interesting to note here the old conversations about women's "voice"—about silence and speech—about coming to "voice." We know that the etiquettes of "good" womanhood are interlaced in that relationship of speech to silence, and what it means to come to speech: literally its tone, its timbre, its pitch. Loudness, and loud women, suggests disruptions and perhaps a transgression of the codes of appropriate and cultivated femininity, one that is clearly racialized and classed.

Here, I must underscore that I am not suggesting that Scripps has explicit rules or codes of silence and quiet—it is just the way the campus operates. Its daily rhythms and temporalities are elegant and restrained. Oddly, unless students are moving to classes, it looks unpeopled. There are only a very few open public places where students gather—a coffee house next to the large cafeteria. Public sociality is contained within limited frames. The silence accentuates the privatization and high individuation of space. It also creates, as I suggest earlier, the racial and class-marked codes of genteel comportment and the terms of dominant white femininity.

There is nothing really surprising about this, I suspect. Any liberal arts college will have its signature rhythms and brand its mission in particular ways. Women's colleges have a particular kind of brand to sell, and they build that within a system of capital in which the material and symbolic are profoundly important. They are also competing hard for students in a dwindling market. This branding, and messaging, presents gendered success and power in quite specific ways: beauty, gentility and a cultivated landscape has an immediate market effect. Wellesley's campus was famous for its beauty too: its lake, the trees with fiery autumn leaves, the winter wonderland when it snowed was breathtakingly lovely.

REFRACTING DOMINANT FEMININITY 3: SHAKING UP CISGENDER MATRICES

There does seem to be a distinct kind of Scripps subject who, ideally, emerges from this landscape. She will be well read and also strive towards leadership and excellence. She too, like the Wellesley Woman, will cultivate this sense and practice of leadership through messages that reflect quite specific experiences, and definitions of entitlement, excellence and exceptionalism.

While there is much we can tease out around these words, I would like to end by thinking of the obvious problematic around cisgender presumptions about leadership and inclusion itself. She is always she. Woman is woman. But four decades of scholarship, activism and advocacy—built on feminist, queer and transgender social movements—must make their mark, and they have. As such, in the past few years, women's colleges have had to think hard about their policies on transgender inclusion in their admissions policy. These debates have raised the most fundamental questions about the foundational purposes of a "women's college," and they have been hugely generative ones.[6]

At Scripps, I witnessed cisgender and transgender students ally together to create a powerful social movement on campus to challenge the admissions policy. They created surveys which showed that most Scripps students were open to transgender students and made powerful arguments to the Board of Trustees. One important one stood out. In the historical moment that women's colleges were created, they were challenging (and continue to challenge) gendered accessibility to education and were built around some understandings of gender justice. To ask for full trans-inclusion follows that logic of gender justice; to not support trans-inclusion is to betray the central premise of why colleges like Scripps and Wellesley were founded.

There are lots of important critiques to add to that one too—that these colleges were founded primarily for wealthy white women and they are also learning to stretch their own horizons because of student-of-color protests around racial and class inclusion. But the question remains, and it is an urgent one: How does an institution premised on gender justice confront attacks against gender justice as well as open itself to non-binary forms of gender? How do we continue to compel our institutions to act courageously, especially as dominant political forces have amplified attacks on intersectional gender freedoms?

The answers to these questions would require some radical revisioning of the structures and governance of neoliberal education itself but since the Seven Sisters, for example, pushed against the powerful mores of their time, why can't we—those of us who are committed to antiracist, queer, transgender and feminist politics—imagine, and build towards, such a possibility? In the meanwhile, political control and governance and the relationship between the three constituencies of power (administration, faculty, and students) have to be reworked through careful bridge-building. It has to be done with an honest reckoning about the limits of mainstream feminism as espoused (implicitly or explicitly) in most elite women's colleges—and how that marginalizes, and excludes, people who don't fit into those terms of feminism, especially in this historical time of open white supremacy and rising intolerance. It requires a revolutionary and transparent relationship to resources and capital—and to capitalism itself.

In other words, it is perhaps time to think not just about "women's colleges" and the corollary that women: feminist has a seamless connection just because you attend a women's college. Indeed, elite women's colleges' investment in dominant cisgender femininity might actually work against a sense of feminisms that is radically and plurally inclusive of people's subjectivities, even if their gender does not fit the older molds of "womanhood." It is time to think of institutions that are explicitly *antiracist feminist* colleges—with a mission statement that fully, and roundly, demarcates the terms of feminisms being espoused—and in which the term "antiracist feminist" is uncompromisingly in its title.

The conversations, and constructions, must continue in unflinching ways. They must unsettle. The white adobe walls suggest conquest as well as beauty. Let's continue to excavate the terms of dominant femininity—and the codes of women's empowerment and leadership—that further its terms. Cultivation engenders violence; beauty can be steeped in cruelty. That is power, certainly. But it is time to imagine power, otherwise.

BIBLIOGRAPHY

Da Costa, Dia. "Academically-Transmitted Caste Innocence." *Raiot: Challenging the Consensus*. Last modified August 24, 2018. Accessed February 2, 2019. http://www.raiot.in/academically-transmitted-caste-innocence/.

Feldman, Kiera. "Opinion: Who Are Women's Colleges For?" *The New York Times*, May 4, 2014. https://www.nytimes.com/2014/05/25/opinion/sunday/who-are-womens-colleges-for.html.

Freitas, Annie. "Beyond Acceptance: Serving the Needs of Transgender Students at Women's Colleges." *Humboldt Journal of Social Relations 1*, no. 39 (2017): 294–314.

Soundararajan, Thenmozhi, and Sinthujan Varatharajah. "Caste Privilege 101: A Primer for the Privileged." *The Aerogram*, February 10, 2015. http://theaerogram.com/caste-privilege-101-primer-privileged/.

The Combahee River Collective. *The Combahee River Collective Statement: Black Feminist Organizing in the Seventies and Eighties*. 1977.

Woodstock School. "History of Woodstock School." Accessed June 27, 2019. http://woodstockschool.in/wp-content/uploads/2016/03/History-of-Woodstock-School.pdf.

NOTES

1. I would like to thank the co-editors, especially Noelle Chaddock, for their immense patience and generosity. I would also like to deeply thank R. A. Justin Joseph (Pomona College '17) for all his help with copyediting this essay on a tight deadline.

2. The Combahee River Collective, *The Combahee River Collective Statement: Black Feminist Organizing in the Seventies and Eighties*, (1977).

3. Thenmozhi Soundararajan and Sinthujan Varatharajah, "Caste Privilege 101: A Primer for the Privileged," *The Aerogram,* February 10, 2015, http://theaerogram.com/caste-privilege-101-primer-privileged/.

4. "History of Woodstock School," Woodstock School, accessed June 27, 2019, http://woodstockschool.in/wp-content/uploads/2016/03/History-of-Woodstock-School.pdf.

5. Dia Da Costa, "Academically-Transmitted Caste Innocence," *Raiot: Challenging the Consensus*, last modified August 24, 2018, accessed February 2, 2019, http://www.raiot.in/academically-transmitted-caste-innocence/.

6. Annie Freitas, "Beyond Acceptance: Serving the Needs of Transgender Students at Women's Colleges," *Humboldt Journal of Social Relations, 1*, no. 39 (2017): 294–314; Kiera Feldman, "Opinion: Who Are Women's Colleges For?" *The New York Times*, May 4, 2014, https://www.nytimes.com/2014/05/25/opinion/sunday/who-are-womens-colleges-for.html.

3

REPO FEM

Timothy W. Gerken

I do not have the lived experiences, academic credentials, nor the specific disciplinary expertise to make a disciplined argument about "the self-proclaimed ownership over the space by those who identify themselves as 'women' or 'feminists,'"[1] however, as a writer and friend, I am concerned about places and spaces, ownership and trespass, fields and fences, form and content, and "hostile, antagonistic relationship(s) for those whose identity expressions and lived experiences do not align"[2] with a majority's position and definition regarding bodily practices and bodily matters. Bodies matter; they come with identities, and identities give us "reasons for doing things."[3] The vagueness of "things" creates opportunities outside or within dichotomies that diffuse restraints. I will be strategizing with vagueness to bring clarity to "problematic shared understandings of the feminine,"[4] with a focus on the Fem.

Our inherited metaphors can be unpredictable or get rather slippery, but they don't warn us with yellow signs saying "SLIPPERY WHEN WET." We mostly accept them as dry and stable. Stability and predictability count on consensus, and consensus historically undervalues matters important to those who live and work and move through and around culturally created edges. Stability and predictability discipline diversity. Binaries and boundaries abandon curiosity and stifle collaborations; "without collaborations, we all die."[5]

The metaphors contested by our collaborators in this volume were inherited and dependent predominantly on visual cues. Our visual acuity—remember that many of us wear glasses—significantly shapes "the world-pictures that determine our standards of thought—the standards by which we judge what is possible and plausible."[6] Biologists now use tools that allow them to clearly see "the great variety of regularly occurring combinations of sex chromosomes and sexual morphology,"[7] which reveal vagueness in birth-designated gender designations as "there are numerous disorders where someone might be male in some of those ways, but female in others."[8] Biologists see and "continue to show that sex is a spectrum,"[9] suggesting "that sex is to some degree produced through the assumptions we make about each other and our bodies, and the meanings we derive from our relationships."[10]

Our relations entangle us in the inherited metaphors used to define us. When we accept these metaphors as our "interpretative framework, we may be said to dwell in them as we do in our own body";[11] however, too often these metaphors become "techniques of alienation."[12] These "techniques have segregated humans and policed identities, obscuring collaborative survival."[13] Those left out of the collaboration because of their adopted metaphors still have to move about society. Their alienation by those with the "right" bodies or who lean right politically or who righteously look to conserve certain places for themselves derives from the assumption that the right metaphors allow us to correctly experience the world, both naturally and culturally.

The categories of nature and culture are muddled, which suggests that any discussion about their importance in determining identity will be messy: "By imagining the pure concepts of nature and culture, we actually produce a large number of objects, processes, experiences, and energies that are neither."[14] The mess leads to falls and slips of tongue. If we listen carefully, or read between the lines, we learn that "most scientists tend to underplay the importance of ambiguity (and the equivocation it invites) in scientific argument; they are wont to insist that they know what they mean."[15] However, "it is only in the closed system of the laboratory that initial conditions can be known, and many natural systems can be described only probabilistically."[16] Some of us thrive in the sterility of the laboratory, but we live in a world with swerve. Our encounters, while often predictable, can lead to engagements "out of which is born something new under the sun."[17] If we "put unpredictable encounters at the center of things,"[18] then we can "cultivate more generous dispositions in oneself by drawing sustenance from the rich abundance of nature/culture."[19] Our abundant interactions counter the "objective penchants of conventional science [which] separate researchers from the phenomena they hope to impart—and in turn separate the readership from the phenomena as well."[20]

The interactions I have collaborated with and assembled in the text that follows attempts to use an abundance of narrative, reading, and writing (fields where I have more experience) "to create a discourse that is rich with the texture of the feminine,"[21] or at least The Fem but not femme (I want to see if I can leave "me" out of it). I recognize that "masculinizing discourses and practices extend beyond male bodies."[22] Here I use Fem, without defining Butch. They exist here without the essence of biology.

> A boyfriend once said that I didn't have a fem bone in my body. They're there, but my fem bones were metaphorically broken and reset during childhood. My father saw my fem. When my hair crossed my ears, "You look like a girl"; when I threw a baseball, "You throw like a girl"; and, when my eyes teared up, "Go ahead, cry like a girl."

I write this as a collaboration between those who know their way around but detour hetero-normative and cisgendered cultural practices. I write "to be everything, in solitude and in exuberance with others" and to discover myself "within the writings of others."[23] I write it as an other.

I write it as a conversation amongst Queens who skirt the status quo by gossiping around it. Gossip bypasses the hierarchy, provides an entry into community, and creates desire. Queens collude with noble passion and see "gossip as both radical and empowering."[24] Gossip is the discourse of Dynasty.

The Queens' power has always been a concern for sociologists, especially male sociologists. For example, psychologist Michael Bailey's text *The Man Who Would Be Queen* was published by the *National Academy of Science* in 2003. Bailey was "intrigued" to meet a male, who was the "most expert cosmetics salesperson at the upscale department store" in his neighborhood.[25] Bailey goes on to gossip:

> Knowing his occupation and observing him briefly and superficially were sufficient, together, for me to guess confidently about aspects of Edwin's life that he never mentioned. I know what he was like as a boy. I know what kind of person he is sexually attracted to. I know what kinds of activities interest him and what kinds do not.
>
> I do not ask Edwin about his childhood because I do not need to. I already know that Edwin played with dolls and loathed football, that his best friends were girls. I know that he was teased by other boys, who called him "sissy." I am fairly certain that his parents did not encourage his feminine behavior, and if I had to bet, I'd say that his father was unhappy about it.[26]

The assuredness suggested by Bailey is disturbing. Whether or not Bailey was correct, his bet goes against the science: "The truth is that you are likely to understand much less about the minds of your family members, friends, neighbors, coworkers, competitors, and fellow citizens than you would guess. One of the biggest barriers to understanding others is excessive egocentrism."[27] We can wonder whether it was Bailey's ego or the ego of his discipline that allows him to be certain. Disciplines revel in their disciplinariness. Queens adore their exuberance. We should celebrate the exuberance of Queens and their defying discourse and behavior. Certainly their gossip about Professor Bailey would not be published by the *National Academy of Science*.

Gossip works. Sociologists mirror its structure: "everyone speaking 'privately' about everybody else" and creating "self-knowledge" that "is both social and personal."[28] However, unlike Bailey's gossip, the Queen's interactions cannot be superficial. Their discourse isn't the behind-the-back gossip the Fem was subject to in school or the gossip published by psychologists; it is the discourse of queer empowerment through shared experiences.

> I liked my friend Frank. When we walked around our elementary school playground during lunch, I would sometimes hold his hand. In this memory, we are in 3rd grade and we are on the little hill that looks down on the field where kids are playing kickball, and the blacktop that we line up on before going back to class. We are in the shade of the three large trees that grow there. We are holding hands; I want to run down the hill while holding his hand: the thrill of doing this together. But, one of the "lunch ladies" as we called them, told

> us that boys don't hold hands. I let go. We walked towards the blacktop. I asked my mom about it when I got home, and she suggested maybe putting my arm around his shoulder was a better idea. It's what boys did. Girls hold hands.

The interactions here are all queer though not all writers are. Queer speech acts expand all discourse and our discourse partners; "queer as a discourse was meant to be inclusive and bridging, while also troubling."[29] This works well with gossip, as "the radical aspect of gossip is that it momentarily undoes social and gendered hierarchies by implicating everyone within the speech community."[30] Examining gossip "one finds both experience and models, but, what's more, the models one finds are not elicited for the benefit of an outsider, but are animated for the benefit of agents themselves."[31] Queens, queers, and fems are all agents in the transgression of convention circumnavigating the roadblocks of constriction. Of course, they are not alone in this struggle.

Writing about the Fem exists, but fem impressions are impossible to sustain: identity has no outside. Biological or psychological behaviors are "utterly intertwined."[32] Fem identity, like all identity, "is negotiated between insiders and outsiders."[33] Fems cohesiveness depends "on the attractiveness" of "the prestige of the group, the members in the group, or the activities in which the group enagages."[34]

Critics see the Fem's wardrobe as stylish but indescribable. Their outfit designed as it's worn and worn inside out. The styles swerve from vintage to futuristic and patterns and fabrics are of the moment. The Fem flashes exuberance. Some may see this as performance, but "it is important to take the banality 'We are all different people' (Axiom 1) very seriously."[35] Eve Sedgewick's Axiom suggests why fems have difficulty expressing what fem is, even to each other: "Every identity has its own distinctive misconceptions."[36] Fems might say "we are trying to use language to express what we feel," but "it is unclear what language does that most effectively."[37] Or, maybe a Fem would say, "I can't own my interpretation, and that is a thrilling thing."[38] Fems also know that "language, no matter how stupid, always leaves someone out."[39]

> While I was in 3rd grade, my sister, who is two years younger, joined a theatre group in our town. She sang and danced. After seeing two of her performances, I asked my mom if I could also join. She said she would ask my dad. My mom and I were in the basement folding

> laundry when she told me what he said: "No son of mine is going to be dancing around on stage. He is going to be outside, playing football." Boys play football.

Fem boys are often left out or worse, singled out. They learn early to "circumvent the intimidation by mesmerizing the bully."[40] The boy being the biggest bully. The boy is something that most boys are. The boy is not a vague notion especially to other boys, especially Fem boys. The Fem absorbs their way through the spaces, structures, and rituals of class, locker rooms, bus rides, and summer vacations with very little to guide them, except the boy and sometimes the girl.

In the 1960s and 1970s psychologists and therapists and researchers were looking to treat the Fem away:

> Young boys with feminine sex-typed behaviors have recently become the object of increased psychological interest, perhaps because of growing evidence that childhood cross-gender manifestations are indicative of later adult sexual abnormalities; e.g., transvestism, transsexualism, or some forms of homosexuality (Green, 1967, 1968; Green and Money, 1961, 1969; Stoller, 1968, 1970). Anatomically normal male children with pronounced feminine characteristics are now diagnosed as having childhood "crossgender identity problems" (e.g., Green, 1968).[41]

Rekers and Lovaas's research was supported by a *United States Public Health Service Research Grant*. This work to hinder homosexuality and gender non-conformity was practiced on children and later used to argue against gay adoption, gay rights, and gay marriage.

> In elementary school during recess we played "kill the guy with the ball" and "smear the queer." Games played by a large group of boys. One boy has the ball and runs and everyone else tries to tackle him and take the ball away. On the playground in 4th grade, I learned that running with a ball and being chased and tackled by a bunch of boys was safer than walking hand in hand with one. Boys kill.

"On manhood: somewhere a little boy makes excuses for the dead bird in his fist":[42] the milieu of maleness begins with the boy or usually the story of the boy. The story of masculinity is a "configuration of practices and discourses that different youths (boys and girls) may embody in different ways and to different degrees."[43] These stories often involve action and adventure: roughhousing boys, kicking up dirt. Boys who do not pursue these hegemonic masculinities suffer, "whereas boys' investment in hegemonic masculinities is the source of power and social approval."[44] Psychologist Jerome Bruner argues that we can characterize a culture "by the narrative models it makes available for describing the course of a life."[45] Narrative models literalize metaphors creating the form and content of expectations: boys and how they are expected to act. Expectations reinforced by social scientists like Bailey or the story disciplined by researchers in the 1970s suggesting "it is an important socialization process for the boy to learn that he will not grow up with the biological possibility of having sexual intercourse with a man."[46]

During the 1980s, certain researchers found the "nontraditional" boy in many fields, and their narratives categorized this nontraditionalist behavior by "descriptive phrases like 'cross-gender identity,' 'feminine sex-typed behavior,' and 'pre-homosexual.' . . . Although they are often used synonymously, each refers to a different type of behavior."[47] Boys learn and achieve masculine behaviors through the "repeated repudiation of the specter of failed masculinity" and by "lobbing homophobic epithets at one another."[48] These behaviors affect all boys: "I remember my high school experiences, specifically calling feminine boys 'faggots,' an act that simultaneous devalued one's manhood and feminine ideals. But in calling fem-boys faggots, I garnered respect from male peers. I showed that I was not a feminine-thus-faggy male but a masculine man. I showed that I could linguistically discipline the feminine, the discursively positioned inferior sex that I, as a masculine man, should desire and dominate."[49] Long before manhood, boys are taught "that faggots were simultaneously predatory and passive and that they were, at all costs, to be avoided."[50] Another method of repudiating the Fem is by adopting Fem behaviors; these enactments "demonstrated that the boy who was invoking the fag was *not* a fag."[51]

> I have always liked clothes. During my first week of junior high, 7th grade, I remember a moment when I was standing in a crush of students in a hallway where all three grades, from the three separate wings, collided. I realized I was the only one wearing red, white, and blue checkered pants and a matching blue turtleneck. All the boys

> and most of the girls had Levi's on. When my mom got home from school, we went shopping. I got two pairs of jeans and Levi cords in 5 different colors. Boys wear jeans.

This is just one side of the story as "little is known about the feelings or sentiments of such a boy on his entrance into a room crowded with belligerent boys who consider him to be the rightful and appropriate target of their aggressiveness."[52] Bullying and creating hostile environments and antagonistic relationships for those that do not practice normative behaviors, while often illegal, continue in our schools and work places. The practice of dominance is part of normative masculinity: "dominance over women and dominance over other, less masculine, men."[53] Bodily practice still seems to be the reason boys, parents, teachers, religious leaders, and therapists attempt to erase the nontraditional boy story. The story of the boy cannot be ambiguous. The boy cannot be vague.

And neither can masculinity. Masculinity needed protection from the "perversion" of homosexuality.[54] As the grand narrative of science took hold in the twentieth century, the story of homosexuality became one of a mental illness with the belief "that homosexuals might be insane."[55] The treatment to "cure" them "included involuntary incarceration and drug and shock therapies, an approach that lasted well into the 1950's."[56]

> Once walking with my mom during a craft fair on Main Street in Smithtown, she introduced me to a colleague who taught kindergarten at her school. He was older. Thinning gray hair and I remember he was wearing a blue blazer even though he was walking through an outdoor craft fair, during summer. After we walked away, my mom said he was "a little light in the loafers." I did not know what she meant. I am not sure why she felt the need to tell me this. I am not certain how old I was though I was probably around 15. I did know how my loafers fit. Gays wear loafers?

Perversion metaphors allowed gays to be seen as subversive, and they became "the target of state-sponsored persecution, homophobia was an absolutely acceptable prejudice."[57] Law enforcement encouraged by the work of Roy Cohn, a gay man who died from AIDS-related causes, and Senator McCarthy joined the crusade against homosexuality by actively searching for and arresting gay men. And, like the fem boy, Fem men were easy targets. Men were "arrested for acting the least bit effeminate" wrote John Kepnar about San Francisco after World War II.[58] The fear of the Fem also worked its way into an internalized homophobia.

One aspect of this homophobia comes from "gay men's anxieties about masculinity, anxieties that had over the decades narrowed the idea of what it meant to look, act like, and be a man."[59] As these men adopted "an implausibly studied machismo," they were also rejecting the "feminized body of the dandy, brought to a peak of perfumed, permed, and blow-dried perfection."[60] The leather scene of the mid to late 1970s worked to stem the Fem as it "enthusiastically conformed to an idealized version of physical manhood—muscles, mustaches, and tight jeans."[61] The S&M leather bars like New York City's Mineshaft had this dress code:

> NO COLOGNE, PERFUME, or STRONG AFTERSHAVE, NO SUITS, TIES, JACKETS, DRESS PANTS, or FANCY SHIRTS, NO DISCO DRAG, NO MAKE-UP OR FEMININE HAIR STYLES, NO FANCY DESIGNER SWEATERS.[62]

Building inclusive spaces for hyper-masculine play and locking the Fem out, unfortunately, did not keep the Fem any safer from the next attempt at erasure.

The AIDS virus is responsible for the death of hundreds of thousands of gay men. The epidemic was mostly ignored by the press through the early 1980s and by President Reagan for the majority of his administration. The epidemic has been touted by many from the religious right (which the Reagan administration counted on for votes) to be a result of the immoral gay lifestyle, "gay male promiscuity, even proof of the inherent unhealthiness of gay sex."[63] Jerry Falwell was famous for his hatred of homosexuality, but in this statement he goes even further: "AIDS is not just God's punishment for homosexuals. It is God's punishment for a society that tolerates homosexuals."[64] Fear of the disease and these new versions of homophobia scared many gay men back into the closet. However, for the Fem, the closet has only been for clothes. The Fem became an easy target as society became more fearful of AIDS and gays.

The AIDS epidemic fostered a change in the dynamics of gay society, which again negatively affected the Fem. Health became a greater concern and with it a new ideal of what was considered sexy. Younger and still "safe" men became fetishized. *Freshman*, a gay porn magazine, introduced "college-aged boys with made-up lips and Brazil-like complexions—not to mention smooth-as-silk arms ornamented with muscle and tendon to die for."[65] Gym culture grew and built up a "rigidly defined physical ideal of 'masculinity.'"[66] The focus on the male body moved from a healthy, natural masculinity to healthy-looking, gym-developed chest, biceps, and abs. Many a fem joined the gym; however, even a muscular Fem would not be embraced by other gay men. These new Fem bodies were also rejected by much of mainstream gay culture as too perfect. The "gym queens," as they became known, "confused gay men who naturally felt they could never measure up to these standards."[67] This led to even more alienation as the focus on physical perfection moved to a focus on bodily practices.

As the internet became more available, and gay chat rooms and meeting sites proliferated, a new self-identifying phrase became popular and more important than just a buff body: "straight-acting." For gay men, the idea of straight-acting "is directly related to how convincingly he is able to present traditionally masculine mannerisms."[68] And, "for whatever reason, masculinity has remained a sexual ideal for a large proportion of gay men."[69] This straight-line singled out the Fem and reinforced our internalized homophobia: "Many gay men refuse to date or be associated with those who are not 'straight acting.' In fact, not only is 'straight' masculinity celebrated on such platforms, but any ostensibly queer identity is subject to homophobic cyber-bullying."[70] Straight-acting "is so markedly offensive because its very existence insists that there is a particular, instantly identifiable manner of being gay (defined by effeminacy)."[71]

The Fems I am most interested in are not interested in strong, at least not in their shoulders and arms, maybe someone else's. They are the models of photographer Ryan McGinley:[72] pretty and sans muscles. The Fem I imagine often self-identifies as a twink: "in gay culture, twinks are young, hairless and skinny men."[73] In other times a dandy, a poof, a sissy, a swish, a queen, a fairy, a fey, a fag. Today's twink is "often, recklessly and unfairly, linked with femininity, vapidity, and submissiveness."[74] However, the Fem does not reject butchness, as it is not a consideration. The Fem may crave butchness in another or maybe more Femness.

> Our high school yearbook has a section called "Senior Superlatives." I was voted "Best Athlete," not "Best Dancer;" that went to Joe S.: Disco Joe. Joe was the first person I knew who died from AIDS-related complications. I really shouldn't say that I knew Joe. I think he transferred to our district before his junior year. We moved along different lines in school, and they did not cross very often. Was that on purpose?

The Fem could have biceps and pecs, but the Fem could not pass as straight. Of course, Fems have no reason to pass for straight, and neither do their straight-acting rejecters. Rejection has been part of gay life. We have been rejected by culture's heteronormativity, and we have used those same beliefs to reject the Fem in an attempt to align ourselves with straight culture. Performing straight masculinity "is something that gay men have struggled with and against for as long as modern gay identities have existed. Because being gay has been so intimately connected with being effeminate."[75] Being effeminate "was—and still is—equated with being submissive, weak and ineffectual."[76] Nothing could be further from the truth.

The Fem brings vagueness and Vegas to the masses, and Vegas is far from ineffectual. Ambiguousness allows confusion: blinding lights, make-up, costumes, chance. Deleuze and Guattari suggest, "Our lives must be indefinite or vague enough to include such potential for other worlds of predictions or individualizations, and so enter into complications with others that are never fully 'explicated.'"[77] Vegas is a queer idea and fuzzy the choice of the Fem and the fugitive. What happens in Vegas stays in Vegas: Carrot Top and Celine and Siegfried and Roy and Cirque du Soleil and roulette and marriage and money. Who do we bet on? What do we see? How do we spend our time? Deleuze and Guattari see vagueness as an opportunity to expand formed identities into multiplicities. Fems live their ideas.

Of course, the Fem is not feminism, nor feminist, nor even feminine, but it leads them all as a prefix and as a way of understanding the movement. Organizations constantly work "to stop or interrupt the movements of deterritorialization, weigh them down, restratify them, reconstitute forms and subjects";[78] an organization, school, or discipline "always concerns the development of forms and the formation of subjects."[79] The Fem is not a subject in need of development. Developing strategies to alienate, exclude, or eliminate the Fem means alienating, excluding, and eliminating femininity and masculinity.

> After graduating from high school, I went to the Coast Guard Academy in New London, CT. One Sunday afternoon—the only day Swabs, freshman, were allowed to leave campus—a few classmates and I walked down to the pizza place and then across the street to the drug store. We were walking around killing time and enjoying our freedom. I stopped in front of the magazine stand, haphazardly picked up a few magazines, and started looking through them. I startled myself when I realized I was looking at a photo of a blonde guy around my age, flexing in front of a pool. He was naked and his erection pointed right at me. For a moment or two, I stared at the photo, saw a few more naked men around the edge of the pool, and then realized what I was looking at. I put the magazine down right away before someone caught me. I had never seen a male porn magazine before. I did not know they even existed. For a while, I thought that drugstore was the only place I could find a magazine like that. It took a few years before I had the courage to buy one for myself.

All of today's subjects, whether masculine, feminine or somewhere else, were formed differently at birth. "We are all the products of someone else's dream,"[80] unaware of how we were supposed to act, until it was too late: we let someone down, we crossed a line, or the lines got blurry. Much to essentialist surprise "no one was born Butch. People were born babies and promptly burst into tears, which was most unbutch."[81] A binary or nonbinary vision of ourselves and or others complicates cultural connections. The complications of these internal categorical conflicts muddle, for "the lines that allow us to find our way, those that are 'in front' of us, also make certain things, and not others, available."[82] Consciousness appreciates the limits of lines as it values control and order. Consensus, control, and order count on boundaries; however, "the boundaries between different categories are often arbitrary, but once some arbitrary boundary exists, we forget that it is arbitrary and get way to impressed with its importance."[83]

The unconscious, however, is less impressed with control and more interested in interruptions. It finds those in the arbitrary, the unavailable, and the unreachable. The unconscious discovers that "when we follow specific lines, some things become reachable and others remain or even become out of reach."[84] The "others" may be subjects that interest us or that we have feelings for, but their blurriness or ours keeps them out of reach. We judge a life of fuzzy lines as lacking "because the disciplines, having gone professional, can only judge what is not already marked for their easy assimilation, as inadequate, unprofessional, even unethical or criminal."[85] The social scientists have their metaphors, and the Fem has more.

Here, the metaphors I celebrate and the lines I attempt to untangle (or maybe tangle is a better verb) are Deleuze and Guattari's "lines of flight."[86] These lines disrupt the disciplined lines: flying away, they wink and flutter and hibernate waiting for that aleatory moment to light a way away from the ways of a hegemonic culture and writing that weighs us down to keep us in-line. Breaking a line or word gives an idea the possibility to become blurry, to rest, and recover from expectations: "poetry is an art of time."[87] Poet Essex Hempel said, "I've always been writing for the long haul."[88] His writing used the "hermeneutics of retrieval" and through this methodology "black queer writers seek to also retrieve those voices that have been marginalized within black queer communities. They seek to rescue the voice of the black 'sissy,' the drag queen, the effeminate black queer."[89] Writing is rescue and retrieval. Maggie Nelson writes "this is what reclaimed terms do—they retain, they insist on retaining, a sense of the fugitive."[90] A poem, for example, "is a methodical working out of fugitive impressions."[91]

Fugitives possess an elusive vision of the renegade. Experts in retrieval and escape; always ready for the knock on the door with a suitcase in the trunk. The most trivial lines come from "children of privilege, who are condemned to know, at all times, where they are positioned—an awareness that squelches the imagination."[92] Imagination absconds the present but lingers in the past and future. It repossesses and retrieves from fields dirtier and less formed than we remember: memory is always constructed and (re)remembered. Writing allows for (re)possession: finding and taking back and owning, and riding with and along and away and around the ideas of others. The writer as a repo man.

Repo Man is a film made by Alex Cox in 1984 starring Emilio Estevez. His character Otto "becomes a repo man not just because he needs money, but because he needs agency and freedom from his parents, his lowlife friends, artificial politics and capitalist factions that require him to wear a uniform, to pick sides."[93] Otto's drift into repoing pushes him away from the binaries of his world: winner or loser, commie or Christian, punk or geek, alien or human, boy or man. As a repo man, he travels in the middle, thus, "the life of the repo man is always intense."[94] Repossessors work space without dividing or picking sides and while trying to remain unseen. Director Alex Cox said *Repo Man* was a film about "maniac cultures" and "repoing people's cars and hating alien ideologies."[95] Roger Ebert concludes that the film "baffles" because "it isn't made from any known formula and it doesn't follow the rules."[96]

One rule that many find baffling is Deleuze's "reading with love":[97] "this intensive way of reading, in contact with what's outside the book . . . getting it to interact with other things, absolutely anything,"[98] requires us to look past and around and through where our eyes have been focused. If we just stare at Estevez, we miss the important business going on at the edge of the screen—the world of the characters—left there by Cox: "Film is a Form in Continuity, within a more or less restricted frame. This frame is its entire world. Nothing exists outside of it. And whatever happens within it is autonomous."[99]

> In 2015 at a LGBTQAI conference in Albany, during a lunch conversation, a female colleague stated that I present as HYPER-MASCULINE (I am not sure she used capitals, but it felt like it to me). I felt a bit uncomfortable. What was she looking at? This concept of masculinity is alluring to many gay men and has provided me some popularity among them. Should I thank my dad? Would he be proud knowing the masculinity he pushed, made me desirable to some men? But why was I uncomfortable? Was I worried she thought it was an act? Is it? Were there not other presentations available for her to comment on or did the location and context allow her to focus on this one: hyper-masculinity?

The Fem identity has no borders, no frames. The Fem has style. To write about the Fem, writers need self-directed readers that "become as interested in the act of writing as in its content: that is, to be as attentive to what the writer is trying to do—how does the writer go about approaching certain lived experiences and why—as in what the writer finds to say about those experiences."[100] As Nussbaum suggested, "Style itself makes its claims, expresses its own sense of what matters."[101]

We seem more comfortable doing this when discussing film and poetry and less when we discuss scholarly work. Commitment to or expectation of a specific structure and a need for transparency makes content the focus in academic writing: every discipline has the ability "to produce its own illusions and to hide behind its own peculiar smoke-screen."[102] American philosopher Richard Rorty ends his book *Achieving Our Country* with this phrase: "It is only those who still read for inspiration who are likely to be of much use in building a cooperative commonwealth."[103] This commonwealth works to expand the edges, allowing more space for more people.

We are defined by our edges: the tip of my tongue, the top of her head, their backside. The edge as a frame confines us. But the edge as opening and as the "what's outside" supports the idea of the multiple, and the conjunction "and" is important when considering all the people we can be and identities we may portray. The *Repo Man* and the other versions *Repo Men* and *Repo Chick* present the edge of cinema, and repos (to be gender neutral) work on the edge. They need to be unnoticed until the engine roars and they speed off. They travel between "owners" (banks and consumers) taking from and using both: they possess the ride and ride the lines between bodies. The journey between points is what matters—the middle, the undefined, the becoming. They (repos and writers and fems) take occupancy in someone else's space and they never own it.

> I wonder about my ways, about my masculine and fem signals. Is my fem in my shoes or my ties or my pattern mixing? Is it the tear in my eye when I hear Spandau Ballet's "True"? Is it my fondness for reminiscing? Or the way my voice lowers during a heated discussion? Are my tattoos my fem? Is my fem my thick salt and pepper beard that I use to attract mates? All of these are me.

This writing is an attempt at finding Fem and (re)becoming Fem. Making up with an idea by Mykel Johnson that to be Fem (Johnson used femme) "is to give honor where there has been shame."[104] Reading someone as fem and butch and masculine and femme and gay and lesbian and bi and trans and cis and straight is fine as long as we don't act through that reading. When we read, we "pick up one tale and produce another."[105] We encounter a roundabout (rather a fork in the road) with numerous opportunities to exit and explore as a new person. A reader on the road to becoming knows "we have a choice of visions and myths we can use to understand the physical world, but we do not have a choice of understanding it without using any myths or visions at all."[106] A successful repo, then, rides the "lines of flight"—the opportunities of multiplicities—rather than sitting in a congestion-stalled identity myth; "we have a real choice between becoming aware of these myths and ignoring them. If we ignore them, we travel blindly inside myths and visions, which are largely provided by other people. This makes it much harder to know where we are going."[107]

The lines we speak, read, and write provide "openings that allow thought to escape from the constraints that seek to define and enclose creativity."[108] The need to define and enclose or erase and arrest the Fem comes from fear: an abusive parent, losing a comfortable position, or a movement across fields. I like that "we write to leave room for interpretation, for misunderstandings, for not knowing."[109] I like that "understanding has never seemed to the point of essays, or of queerness."[110] This queer essay remains loyal to The Fem, to vague, to blaze, to swerve and to the access and accessories they promise.

Fem is the firefly. Flashing over the grassy field looking for a mate. It blazes. It disappears. Fireflies disrupt the night and expand the field. They interrupt the obscure and brighten the obvious. The firefly is born glowing: it is innate. Their glow keeps them safe below ground, so they have a chance to light up the night sky. Their brilliance attracts mates and our attention. In the dark their visual signals part their multiplicity and "may also play a role in creating new species."[111] With over two thousand species, there are a lot of ways to be a firefly.

There are a lot of ways to be a man and a lot of ways to be a woman and a lot of road in between those destinations. There is also no biological reason to be either one. This text's goal was to work with "a discourse that is rich with the texture of" the Fem,[112] and it suggests that we allow the edges of our fields to grow past where we thought they ended. Repoing Fem lets us take back the past and drive the future; it expands the opportunities for building that cooperative commonwealth

Rorty suggests. It is a move towards "increasing sensitivity, increasing responsiveness to the needs of a larger and larger variety of people and things."[113]

I light up when I read Tisa Bryant: "Let us write writing. Let us have vibrancy, and exuberance and excess. Let us be everything."[114]

NOTES

1. Personal communication: language from the *Call for Papers* for this collection.
2. Personal communication: language from the *Call for Papers* for this collection.
3. Appiah, *Lies That Bind*, 9.
4. Personal communication: language from the *Call for Papers* for this collection.
5. Tsing, *Mushroom at the End*, 28.
6. Midgley, *Science as Salvation*, 15.
7. Appiah, *Lies That Bind*, 13.
8. Sapolosky, "Caitlyn Jenner and Our Cognitive Dissonance," 4.
9. Ainsworth, "Sex Redefined," 291.
10. Addison, "Human Sex Is Not Simply," para. 11.
11. Polanyi, *Personal Knowledge: Towards*, 60.
12. Tsing, *Mushroom at the End*, 19.
13. Tsing, *Mushroom at the End*, 19.
14. Bennett, *Enchantment of Modern Life*, 96.
15. Keller, *Mirage of a Space*, 12.
16. Bennett, *Enchantment of Modern Life*, 102.
17. Bennett, *Enchantment of Modern Life*, 100.
18. Tsing, *Mushroom at the End*, 20.
19. Bennett, *Enchantment of Modern Life*, 110.
20. Anderson, "Embodied Writing and Reflections," 84.
21. Personal communication: language from the *Call for Papers* for this collection.
22. Pascoe, *Dude, You're a Fag*, 9.
23. Bryant, "To Be Everything," 47.
24. Roulston, "Discourse, Gender, and Gossip," 58.
25. Bailey, *Man Who Would Be Queen*, ix.
26. Bailey, *Man Who Would Be Queen*, ix.
27. Epley, "Why We Can't Get," paras. 2–3.

28. Roulston, "Discourse, Gender, and Gossip," 55.
29. Martin, "Interview With," 3.
30. Roulston, "Discourse, Gender, and Gossip," 56.
31. Besnier, "The Politics of Emotion," 237.
32. Sapolosky, *Behave: The Biology of Humans*, 5.
33. Appiah, *Lies That Bind*, 79.
34. Festinger, "Informal Social Communication," 274.
35. During, *Cultural Studies*, 320. During points out that Sedgewick refers to both the difference between individuals and how individuals are continuously changing, so always different.
36. Appiah, *Lies That Bind*, xvi.
37. Butler, "Gender Performance," 4.
38. Wang, "Interview With," 17.
39. Als, *White Girls*, 162.
40. Koestenbaum, *My 1980's*, 237.
41. Rekers and Lovaas, "Behavioral Treatment of Deviant," 173.
42. Araguz, *Book of Flight*, 20.
43. Pascoe, *Dude, You're a Fag*, 5.
44. Morojele, "What Does It Mean," 689.
45. Bruner, "Life as Narrative," 694.
46. Rekers, "Typical Gender Development," 566.
47. Coleman, "Nontraditonal Boys: A Minority," 253.
48. Pascoe, *Dude, You're a Fag*, 5.
49. Adams and Jones, "Telling Stories: Reflexivity," 621–22.
50. Pascoe, *Dude, You're a Fag*, 53.
51. Pascoe, *Dude, You're a Fag*, 60. Italics by author.
52. Kama, "Effeminophobia and Pephobia," 90.
53. Pascoe, "Who Is a Real Man?," 123.
54. Fone, *Homophobia: A History*, 10.
55. Fone, *Homophobia: A History*, 10.
56. Fone, *Homophobia: A History*, 10.
57. Fone, *Homophobia: A History*, 10.
58. Sadownick, *Sex Between Men*, 44.
59. Signorile, *Life Outside*, 38.
60. Harris, *Rise and Fall*, 95.
61. Signorile, *Life Outside*, xix.
62. Fritscher, "Introduction to the Academy," 484.
63. Rotello, *Sexual Ecology*, 1.
64. Smith, "AIDS and Activism," para. 11.
65. Sadownick, *Sex Between Men*, 188.
66. Signorile, *Life Outside*, 32.

67. Sadownick, *Sex Between Men*, 215.
68. Michelson, "If You Think 'Straight-Acting,'" para. 6.
69. Rotello, *Sexual Ecology*, 41.
70. Al-Kadhi, "Problem with Straight-Acting," para. 1.
71. Michelson, "If You Think 'Straight-Acting,'" para. 6.
72. McGinley is a photographer whose early work often focused on young men and women who were lean and "pretty" out playing the world. McGinley once suggested that he hated muscles.
73. Staples, "As a Gay Man," para. 11.
74. Kornhaber, "What the Age of Twink," para. 7.
75. Michelson, "If You Think 'Straight-Acting,'" para. 7.
76. Michelson, "If You Think 'Straight-Acting,'" para. 7.
77. Rajchman, *Deleuze Connections,* 84.
78. Deleuze and Guattari, *A Thousand Plateaus*, 270.
79. Deleuze and Guattari, *A Thousand Plateaus*, 265.
80. Als, *White Girls,* 206.
81. Henley, *The Butch Manual,* 12.
82. Ahmed, *Queer Phenomenology: Orientations,* 14.
83. Sapolosky, *Behave: The Biology of Humans*, 6.
84. Ahmed, *Queer Phenomenology: Orientations*, 14.
85. Clough and Halley, *Affective Turn*, 28.
86. Deleuze and Guattari, *A Thousand Plateaus*.
87. Ali, "Interview with Kazim," 33.
88. Hemphill, *Muses from Chaos and Ash*, 244.
89. Sneed, *Representations of Homosexuality*, 111.
90. Nelson, *Argonauts*, 29.
91. Paglia, *Break, Blow, Burn*, xiv.
92. Als, *The Women*, 76.
93. Tafoya, "Repo Man (1984)," 2.
94. Cox, *Repo Man,* 1984.
95. Cox, "Directing," para. 16.
96. Ebert "Reviews: *Repo Man*," para. 1.
97. Deleuze, *Negotiations: 1972–1990*, 9.
98. Deleuze, *Negotiations: 1972–1990*, 8–9.
99. Myers, "Sidney Myers," para. 21.
100. Lu, "Reading the Personnel," 54.
101. Nussbaum, *Love's Knowledge*, 3.
102. Deleuze and Guattari, *What Is Philosophy?*, 6.
103. Rorty, *Achieving Our Country*, 104.
104. Johnson, "Butchy Femme," 396.
105. Schlesinger, "Exiles and Ethnographers," 71.

106. Midgley, *Science as Salvation*, 13.

107. Midgley, *Science as Salvation*, 13.

108. Deleuze and Guattari, *What Is Philosophy?*, viii.

109. Adams and Jones, "Mothers, Faggots, and Witnessing," 108.

110. Fleischmann, *Body Forms: Queerness*, viii.

111. Monahan, "Animals That Glow for Sex," para. 1. Research suggests that glowing animals are more likely to create a new species.

112. Personal communication: language from the *Call for Papers* for this collection.

113. Rorty, *Philosophy and Social Hope*, 81.

114. Bryant, "To Be Everything," 49.

4

WHITE INNOCENCE AS A FEMINIST DISCOURSE

Intersectionality, Trump, and Performances of "Shock" in Contemporary Politics

Sara Salem

Donald Trump's victory in the 2016 US presidential elections was met with a wide range of emotion, from shock and anxiety to condemnation and anger, both across the country and in other parts of the world. Take Sara Benincasa's piece for The Nation, where she writes: "Part of my unrelenting sadness is a kind of narcissism that I need to get over: How could I get everything so wrong? Even worse, I feel like I'm part of the problem. I'm the kind of optimistic liberal feminist, maybe a tad bit on the self-congratulatory side."[1] Or Michelle Goldberg for Slate: "Obviously, I was very wrong. Instead of the year that the highest glass ceiling shattered, 2016 might go down as the year the feminist bubble burst. In America, men have always ruled, and right now I wonder if they always will."[2] Bonds of sisterhood and solidarity were apparently thrown under the bus by this 53 percent of women, who saw fit to vote for a candidate who was so clearly sexist. This is in comparison to 96 percent of Black women who voted for Clinton. Clearly, something had gone very wrong.

Since Trump's victory, the affective response of shock has only intensified. I have become increasingly interested in the role of "shock" in contemporary responses to political events. Almost every day, we hear of people's reactions to politics take shape in the form of shock, surprise, horror, anger, helplessness or apathy. Similarly, gains made by far-right parties and politicians across Europe, Asia and Latin America—most recently Brazil—also elicit responses of shock. All of these reveal important points about our contemporary juncture and the ways in which we understand past, present and future. And yet, for people living under imperial and neo-imperial conditions, under severe economic strain, under racialised forms of violence, and under patriarchal and heteronormative structures of societal organisation—shock was not necessarily the only reaction; often anger, dismay, and a whole host of other responses were articulated. Alongside these, there was often the expression of "unsurprised"—the notion that while what is happening may be shocking, it isn't really surprising.

However, the emotion of shock in particular is especially revealing, I believe, of something Gloria Wekker calls "white innocence." I'm interested in the performance of innocence that is embedded within shock/surprise, and the ways in which it often reveals a willful ignorance of the realities of race, empire, nation and gender that have produced our modern world order. In other words, what does being shocked today mean, given the presence of work and activism that has for so long pointed to the troubling reality of our postcolonial condition? Who has the privilege of being shocked? And how does "shock" function as a way of further deflecting issues of race and empire?

There is little doubt that parts of the US electorate are satisfied with the outcome of the election and its aftermath, in particular groups that have retrospectively been labelled as responsible for Trump's victory.[3] This chapter, however, looks at a different emotional response to the election result by focusing on a group—liberal feminists—that expressed shock at both the outcome and the wide support Trump received from white women.[4] Indeed one of the most noted features of the election outcome within feminist circles was the proportion of white American women that voted for Trump over Hillary Clinton—said to be around 53 percent.[5] It is this statistic—perhaps even more than the election victory itself—that has caused immense shock and disappointment amongst liberal feminists. In this chapter, I revisit two historical moments in order to trace the ways in which Black feminists on the one hand and Arab feminists on the other—in different times and spaces—articulated the problems with a white, liberal feminism that did not take race and empire seriously. Looking at Sojourner Truth's *Ain't I a Woman* speech and the debates Egyptian feminists had around Palestine, I show that there are important lessons in history for white, liberal feminists to learn about the intertwining of racism, capitalism and empire in the making of today's world.

Writing as a non-American academic, I see this intervention as part of an attempt to globalise contemporary US events, which often tend to be analysed parochially. The reality of the US as the current imperial power means that US elections have extremely wide ramifications at the international level. This alone suggests why it is important to analyse them. However, another reason for choosing to look at this particular moment and argue that a global lens is needed is because it is only by historicising US liberal feminism and its ties to imperialism that the shock expressed by many feminists can be tied to white innocence: a concept based on Gloria Wekker's book by the same name, which implies being colour-blind, seeing the self as ethical and moral, and, importantly, positing the self as non-racist, perhaps even anti-racist—all the while actively engaging in racialized projects of domination. Exploring feminism through a global lens and centring global histories of feminism would shed light on the very structural realities that played a role in Trump's election victory, including racism and imperialism. Such an exploration, and familiarity with these global structural realities, may have in turn prevented shock from being the dominant form of response on the part of liberal feminists. It is only through willful ignorance that the central role of race in determining political outcomes could have been ignored. This in turn suggests that feminism of a certain type—white, liberal feminism—shares some of the burden of having contributed to the election of Donald Trump. The hegemony of this type of feminism at the expense of more radical feminist project on the one hand, as well as the absence of a race critique in much of white, liberal feminism that could have done the political work of demobilising women who voted for Trump on the other, suggest a need to pay attention to the role of certain strands of feminism and the societies they contribute to creating.

The aim of this chapter is thus to probe the shock many feminists articulated as a response to this statistic. Should we allow the shocked response itself to be of equal interest as the original statistic to intersectional feminist debates? I argue that placing these events within both a global and historical frame suggests that the shock felt by many was not as innocent as it appeared to be. By addressing two historical events, I ask why this particular statistic was a shock to many (in particular, white, liberal feminists), and what assumptions underlie this response. I look back at these historical events because they were moments—both over one hundred years ago—during which the absences and limitations of white, liberal feminism were clearly articulated by Black women on the one hand and Arab women on the other. These absences were seen as problematic because they limited the radical ways in which feminists imagined they could transform societies they were part of. I also look back at these historical events because had these interventions been taken seriously, feminists across geographic, temporal and cultural spaces may have taken more seriously the contention that our modern moment is deeply imbued with racism, capitalism and imperialism. In other words, events such as the election of Donald Trump, his many acts while in office, as well as the rise of the far right across the world from Hungary to the Netherlands, from Brazil to India, would not be "shocking" but rather unsurprising.

The first historical event is the debate around Sojourner Truth's speech in 1831 at the Ohio Women's Rights Convention entitled *Ain't I a Woman*, and in particular the responses from white feminists at the time. The second historical event is a debate around Palestine within the Egyptian feminist movement in the 1920s that caused Egyptian feminists to turn away from organising with British and American feminists and instead forge alliances with African and Arab feminists. This followed disagreements about the occupation of Palestine in particular and imperialism in general. I use these two events to contextualize the decision by so many white women in our contemporary moment to vote for Trump, as well as the resulting (white feminist) shock following this. These two events not only articulate a clear critique of white, liberal feminism that highlights its absences, but also articulate a conception of the global order as one built on racism, capitalism and empire. This global order is precisely one that *can* produce Trumps, Bolsonaros, Netanyahus or Modis; in other words, this is a global order within which far-right racist forms of politics are not shocking but almost inevitable if not resisted. This is in distinction to ideas of the global order articulated by white, liberal feminists that did not always centre race and empire as central configurations of power, and thus constructed ideas of the global order within which the appearance of far-right racist forms of politics *are* unexpected.

Gloria Wekker's recent work on white innocence[6] underlies my questions surrounding both sides of the spectrum of white feminism: on the one hand, the guilt displaced by white, liberal feminists onto women who voted for Trump (a guilt the women who voted may not have felt at all), and on the other hand, the innocence on the part of feminists who did not believe it possible that so many white women would vote for Trump. In addition, I engage intersectionality as a framework for understanding the dominance of some social categories over others at given moments in time. Intersectionality pushes feminist scholars to ask what has been left out of the stories we tell, which experiences are valued, and what types of solutions exist to the continuing problems faced by marginalised groups globally, and within academia. I argue that intersectionality is also a useful framework for tracing the dominance of some social categories and experiences over others in certain moments. While we all experience multiple social categories simultaneously, there is something to be said for the context we find ourselves in at any given moment may bring one category to prominence—in other words, I want to explore Dubravka Zarkov's suggestion that there are "master cateories" in intersectional analysis; categories that dominate experience during certain moments.[7] I ask whether this is a useful approach in understanding why such a high proportion of white American women voted for Trump, and suggest that at that particular moment in contemporary American history, race—along with racism—was the master category defining the experiences of many white American women, rather than gender. However, I also argue that understanding the resulting shock on the part of white feminists *at the statistic itself* also suggests the dominance of race, for had they been more attuned to the intersections of race, gender and nation in American society, perhaps shock would not have been the dominant response. Here I draw on responses from Black feminists as well as feminists in the Global South who responded with anger and disappointment, but not shock.

Reading this statistic and responses to it through the two historical events mentioned above allows me to suggest that the shock expressed by many feminists becomes questionable when we look at the history of how race and gender have intersected both within the US and globally. I further suggest that using intersectionality as well as Wekker's concept of white innocence provides a constructive and innovative approach to understanding the continuing dominance of race within feminist work, both inside and outside of academia. The first section of the chapter looks at the two historical events in detail: on the one hand, the debates around Sojourner Truth's *Ain't I a Woman* in the late 1800s and early 1900s, and in particular responses from white feminists; and on the other the debates among Egyptian feminists in the early 1900s that ultimately led to their turn away from organising with Western feminists. The second section explores Gloria Wekker's notion of white innocence, relating it back to the two historical moments, and argues that it is a useful framework with which to understand contemporary events. The third section brings the concept of white innocence in conversation with intersectionality, and in particular the idea of master categories. The final section ties together the historical moments and the theoretical concepts in order to probe the feelings of shock felt by many liberal feminists at the large proportion of white American women that voted for Donald Trump.

AIN'T I A WOMAN?

This section explores Sojourner Truth's speech *Ain't I a Woman*, and the ways in which we can see the beginnings of white innocence among white liberal feminists in the claims made by Truth. By extending Gloria Wekker's concept of white innocence—expanded on further in the chapter—I argue that movements based on the tenets of liberalism exhibit white innocence, namely: "not seeing colour," seeing the self as ethical and moral, and, importantly, positing the self as non-racist, perhaps even anti-racist. Sojourner Truth gives this famous speech to anti-abolition groups, among them white feminists who were fighting to end slavery. It is here that the comments she makes are interesting to note, as it shows the limits of the white, liberal feminist project when it comes to race. The following section charts a similar debate in a different context: Egypt in the 1920s and 1930s under British occupation. Here we see another disconnection between feminists of colour and white feminists over imperialism, in this case in the context of Palestine. On the one hand, Sojourner Truth's speech shows the limits of white liberal feminism in terms of race, and on the other hand the debates among Egyptian feminists show the limits of white liberal feminism in terms of imperialism.

Sojourner Truth's now-famous speech was originally given at the Women's Convention in Akron, Ohio, on the 29th of May 1851. Truth's speech was directed to both men and white women, representing an instance of a double critique. On the one hand, through questions about what it is precisely that sets women apart from men and "justifies" their inferior status, she asks:

> Then that little man in black there, he says women can't have as much rights as men, 'cause Christ wasn't a woman! Where did your Christ come from? Where did your Christ come from? From God and a woman! Man had nothing to do with Him.

On the other hand, she addresses white women, to whom she asks more directly the question: "Ain't I a woman?" It is this question that brings to the surface the exclusions of the American feminist movement, exclusions that have continued to haunt it until today. By asking what exactly qualifies women as women, Truth points to race as a characteristic that serves to cut lines between women; to render some more deserving of womanhood than others.

Writing later, bell hooks explains that in using the term "Ain't I a woman," she is referencing a universal experience shared by Black American women.[8] It is this experience that Sojourner Truth alludes to in her speech; the experience of being excluded from the universal, and through that the experiencing of a different type of universalism, that of Black womanhood. This speech is an important historical event because of the ways in which it points to a foundational myth of liberal feminism: that of its supposed universalism. Postcolonial, Black and Third World feminists have all deconstructed this myth, thereby provincializing liberal feminism and returning it back to its white, Euro-American middle-class roots.[9] Despite this deconstruction, and the tonnes of ink spilled on questions of race within feminism, the question continues to haunt feminism today. Recent uses of women's rights to justify imperialist adventures in Iraq and Afghanistan, discriminatory laws against Muslim women in France, as well as the role feminism has played in justifying carceral technologies that lock up Black men in the US, show that feminists are far from innocent when it comes to questions of justice for all women.[10] This haunting repeatedly resurfaces during particular events.

What is interesting about Sojourner Truth's question is that it is ultimately directed at both white men and women; uniting them racially. Her question—*Ain't I a woman?*—asked both the white men and white women present why she was not considered to be a woman. This was one of the first critiques of white feminism, and it was taking place in the heart of one of the most racialized systems of oppression the world has ever known. It is this question that frames postcolonial and Black feminist critiques of liberal white feminism, by pointing at a simple fact: we are not all considered to be equally women. This simple fact is what ultimately brings down the house of cards: for if equality does not exist among women, how can we take seriously a movement that is based on calls for equality among all human beings?

The following section demonstrates this same contradiction again, on the other side of the world. Ultimately it is the question of who counts as a woman that has consistently undone the white liberal feminist project. Understanding white liberal feminist support for projects of colonisation—internal or external—ranging from their support of the British colonial project to current support for burqa bans in Europe—touches once again on the question of who counts as a woman and is therefore deserving of gender equality. Colonialism and slavery as two connected projects of Euro-American domination dispossess, subjugate and often exterminate whole populations and in general are premised on extreme forms of violence. This affects women as well as men, and historically has required the dehumanisation of these populations on the part of colonisers and slaveholders. This dehumanisation was very much a gendered process, and women often played a role in this, bringing us back to the question: Aren't they women? This echoes important critiques of white, liberal feminism by feminists of colour who have shown how the category of womanhood—although presented as neutral—is often racialised and classed.[11] In the following case, Palestinian women, for example, are not seen as worthy of support beyond their status as victims of (Palestinian male) patriarchy. The absence of imperialism means that debates among liberal feminists were not only incomplete but also served to further disempower feminists who did take seriously the intersections of empire, race, gender, class, and nation.

IMPERIALISM, FEMINISM, AND THE OCCUPATION OF PALESTINE

Shifting context, this section looks at some of the disagreements between Egyptian and Western feminists in the 1920s and 1930s, specifically over colonialism and the colonisation of Palestine, in order to further historicise the fraught trajectory white feminism travelled as it began engaging with transnational feminist networks. The contradictions between pushing for universal gender equality while ignoring the reality of colonialism were what eventually led to a break in relations between Egyptian feminists active in the early twentieth century and their Western feminist counterparts.

Starting in the late 1800s after the establishment of the printing press and rise in literacy rates in Egypt, there emerged a vibrant feminist movement with notable personalities, including Huda Sha'arawi, Nabawiya Moussa, Malak Hifni Nassef, and Saiza Nabarawi. This movement, greatly inspired by modernist ideas of progress, pushed for women's right to work and education, greater choice in marriage and divorce, as well as the abolishing of seclusion and forced veiling. These issues collectively became known as the "woman question."[12] The class background of many of these feminists can help in explaining both their reliance on modernist ideas, as well as the fact that they spoke numerous languages and travelled widely. Indeed it is these two factors that allowed them to visit Europe often, and forge connections to both European and American feminists. It is these connections that form the subject of this section.

The expansion of British colonialism, particularly through capitalist development, began to have dramatic ramifications on Egypt, as Egypt's political and economic system became increasingly redirected towards British needs. For the feminist movement, Egyptian independence was seen as inextricably tied to gender equality. This understanding of gender equality was what ultimately led to tensions between Egyptian and Western feminists, specifically over European colonialism in general and the colonisation of Palestine in particular. It was claimed that Western feminists were not putting in practice the democratic principles that they consistently spoke of and encouraged.[13]

Egyptian feminists also began to note the double standard at play in the realm of international politics. They pointed out, for example, that countries such as Britain were never criticised for colonial rule or the giving away of Palestine, whereas countries deemed "undemocratic" such as Egypt were constantly criticised. At a feminist congress in Copenhagen, there was an explosive confrontation surrounding the myth of a "global sisterhood." Margot Badran writes:

> This double standard made Huda Sha'arawi feel that "it had become necessary to create an Eastern feminist union as a structure within which to consolidate our forces and help us to have an impact upon the women of the world." Indeed as early as 1930 Nabarawi had asserted that the path toward liberation of Eastern women was different than that of Western women, suggesting that Eastern women should unite. Meanwhile a move toward Arab unity had been growing among women and men in Egypt and other Arab countries.[14]

Not all Western feminists were comfortable addressing the problem of imperialism, and this is ultimately what led to Egyptian feminists looking elsewhere for solidarity.[15] Eventually they were to turn towards African and Asian feminists and create separate conferences that focused on issues affecting colonised nations. The reluctance of Western feminists to speak out against the Balfour Declaration and the subsequent colonisation of Palestine was the final straw for Egyptian feminists, who did not see a separation between gender justice and national liberation. In an instance of colonisation, they saw feminism's role as one of resistance; feminists were supposed to challenge all forms of oppression, rather than focus on gender, as though it was neatly separable from other forms of oppression. Alongside this was the obvious problem of Western feminist support for these very colonial projects. Returning to the question posed by Sojourner Truth, we again see that for women supporting colonial projects, colonised women simply were not deserving women. The category of "woman" has always been an already-racialized category that is far from universal, even as it was claimed to be so.

In both this instance and the previous example of Sojourner Truth, we can already see an understanding of intersectionality; the idea that gender as a single category can never and has never told a complete story. For Truth, race and the experience of slavery was very much part of her gendered experiences; for the Egyptian feminists, colonialism and nationalism were part and parcel of gender justice. We also see the clear absences in their theorisations of inequality that were already hampering the ability of white liberal feminists to forge transnational or cross-racial solidarities: the inability to take racism and imperialism seriously. Rather than see gender as constituted through various structures, the tendency was—and often continues to be—to understand women's experiences as being first and foremost about gender. This erases other structures such as racism and capitalism that produce differing realities of gender inequality, which in turn reproduces problematic power dynamics within the feminist movement.

WHITE INNOCENCE

Gloria Wekker's ground-breaking book, *White Innocence*, explores the Dutch colonial cultural archive in order to demonstrate the ways in which whiteness has been central to the construction of the modern Netherlands as a nation. She takes the concept of a cultural archive from Edward Said, a concept he uses to foreground the centrality of imperialism to Western culture. Wekker argues that the Dutch self was essentially created through a "racial grammar, a deep structure of inequality in thought and affect based on race," which was installed in nineteenth-century European imperial populations.[16] She writes, summarising the book:

> This book is dedicated to an exploration of a strong paradox that is operative in the Netherlands and that, as I argue, is at the heart of the nation: the passion, forcefulness and even aggression that race, in its intersections with gender, sexuality, and class, elicits among the white population, while at the same time the reactions of denial, disavowal and elusiveness reign supreme. I am intrigued by the way that race pops up in unexpected places and moments, literally as the return of the repressed, while a dominant discourse stubbornly maintains that the Netherlands is and always has been colour-blind and antiracist, a place of extraordinary hospitality and tolerance toward the racialized/ethnicized other, whether this quintessential other is perceived as black in some eras or Muslim in others.[17]

The concept of white innocence itself is defined by Wekker in relation to the Netherlands: "With the title White Innocence, I am invoking an important and apparently satisfying way of being in the world. It encapsulates a dominant way in which the Dutch think of themselves, as being a small, but just, ethical nation; thus free of racism; as being inherently on the moral and ethical high ground, thus a guiding light to other folks and nations."[18] While Wekker explicitly applies this concept to the Netherlands and other nations with an imperial history, I want to posit that it also applies to liberal feminists, both historically and contemporarily. Because the Netherlands is a strongly liberal nation, where liberalism is a central aspect of the self, I posit that there is something in liberalism itself that leads to the construction and reproduction of white innocence as a means of deflecting claims of racism. By extension, this would suggest that movements based on the tenets of liberalism may also exhibit white innocence, namely: not seeing colour; seeing the self as ethical and moral, and, importantly, positing the self as non-racist, perhaps even anti-racist—all the while actively engaging in racialized projects of domination. In the case of liberal feminism in the US and the responses of liberal feminists to the election of Donald Trump, these features appear and reappear, and suggest that the shock many of these feminists felt was only possible because of both their active inattentiveness to race and imperialism as well as the use of innocence to detract away from liberal feminism's role in perpetuating the racial project in the US. Innocence is therefore two-sided: it is an active inattentiveness that leads to the supposedly innocent ignorance that is part and parcel of white innocence; and at the same time it is a deflection away from the role liberalism has played in colonial and racial projects of domination by making claim to innocence.

While nations such as the Netherlands are able to construct themselves through white innocence because of the hegemony of liberalism within the nation itself, the context of the United States is different. Instead, we see that liberal hegemony does not exist and that there remains fierce competition over the identification of the American self and the American nation. This returns us to the question of the move to blame the white working class in the US for the election of Trump, thus creating a binary between progressive, liberal Americans (usually in major cities in the North), and a regressive conservative majority (usually in the South, and often in smaller towns). It is thus within the liberal part of the nation that we see the characteristics Wekker speaks of, including a tendency to see oneself as already anti-racist.

The intertwining of ignorance and innocence is particularly interesting—what is it that separates one from the other? Wekker writes: "The claim of innocence is a double-edged sword: it contains not-knowing, but also not wanting to know, capturing what philosopher Charles W. Mills has described as the epistemology of ignorance (1997, 2007)."[19] This innocence is often performed in the Netherlands (and other European countries) by displacing racism onto the US.[20] Within the US, however, this innocence is performed by displacing racism onto specific demographics, namely the white working class and Americans from the "South." This has resulted in a narrative that posits American racism as something only found in certain places among certain people. It is precisely this move that constructs liberal Americans as non-racist, and by extension, innocent. It is important to note that innocence is an active process; it cannot function as a means of exonerating liberal racism. Not-knowing on the one hand, and displacing on the other, are both active movements that work to detract attention away from liberalism's role in the reproduction of racism. Histories of American white supremacy—often told through the lens of the "South"—are also histories of liberal white supremacy. Similarly, histories of colonialism as a form of white supremacy must take into account the role of liberalism in constituting this racialized form of domination. Because liberalism has never come to terms with this role, white innocence has emerged as the latest means of deflecting responsibility towards other groups. This innocence is not defensible—in fact, it is not even innocent. To remain innocent means to remain in ignorance; and this is a wilful, active process, not an innocent, passive one.

The reasons behind this innocence are important to probe, and the one I focus on here is that of the unwillingness to confront past and present imperialism, including the extermination of Native Americans, the transatlantic slave trade, and the (too) many wars that have characterised US foreign policy since then, as well as the racialized political system that continues to kill (literally and metaphorically) non-white—and in particular Black—bodies today. Scholars have shown that liberal Americans have not been excluded from such projects, and in many instances have been the driving forces behind them.[21] Indeed liberalism has been part and parcel of imperialism from the very start.[22] Liberal feminism in particular has played a constitutive role in the gendered justifications used for empire and occupation.[23] Building on this, the following section brings together the historical moments discussed previously with the concept of white innocence, in order to suggest that an intersectional approach that privileges certain categories at certain moments in time can shed light on how liberal feminist shock at the election of Donald Trump is nothing shocking in and of itself, but follows an older historical trajectory.

MASTER CATEGORIES AND WILFUL IGNORANCE

The response from feminists—and in particular liberal feminists—to the election of Donald Trump in 2016 was overwhelmingly one of shock, alongside disappointment and fear. In a piece for *New York Magazine* entitled "Shattered," Rebecca Traister writes: "The resounding, surprising, data-defying victory of a man who ran on open racism and misogyny, and was voted into office by 63 percent of white men and 53 percent of white women voters, was made possible by voters threatened by the increased influence of women and people of color."[24] Further on, she notes: "Tears, for women, only sometimes express sadness and vulnerability. Just as often, they signal rage," highlighting the intense emotional response to the election results among many women.[25] Gloria Steinem commented: "Never again is anyone going to say 'post-feminist' or 'post-racist' because we [now] understand that there is something like a third of the country that is still locked into these old hierarchies."[26] Susan Chira in the *New York Times* wrote: "This was supposed to be the year of triumph for American women. A year that would cap an arc of progress: Seneca Falls, 1848. The 19th Amendment, 1920. The first female American president, 2017. An inauguration that would usher in a triumvirate of women running major Western democracies. Little girls getting to see a woman in the White House. Instead, for those at the forefront of the women's movement, there is despair, division and defiance. Hillary Clinton's loss was feminism's, too."[27] She goes on to note: "A majority of white women voted for him, shattering myths of female solidarity and the belief that demeaning women would make a politician unelectable."[28] Furthermore, "In these postelection conversations, the rawest wounds were expressed by black women who felt betrayed by white women's support for Mr. Trump. These women worry that the national chest-beating about identity politics and the resolve to win back the white working class will come at their expense, subordinating issues of racial justice."[29]

Susan Faludi, in the *Democracy Journal*, writes: "So many feminists, myself included, were blindsided."[30] Sam Smethers, chief executive at the Fawcett Society, told *Newsweek* that "women all over America now have to focus on defending their rights and freedoms. We have to ask ourselves how it's possible that someone who bragged about sexually assaulting women has become the most powerful politician in the world."[31] Michelle Goldberg for Slate: "Obviously, I was very wrong. Instead of the year that the highest glass ceiling shattered, 2016 might go down as the year the feminist bubble burst. In America, men have always ruled, and right now I wonder if they always will."[32] Joan Walsh writes in The Nation: "I've worn the same t-shirt to bed since the night of the election. It says, 'When they go low, we go to the White House.' The writer Sara Benincasa produced them, an obvious homage to Michelle Obama's stirring, 'When they go low, we go high.' I bought it for my daughter, who worked her heart out for Hillary Clinton for more than a year, in five different states. Obviously, given Donald Trump's devastating win, I couldn't give it to my daughter. I can't imagine wearing it outside the house. I was wrong, so very wrong. And so were you, Sara, and Michelle, and yes Hillary, you too."[33]

I am especially struck by Gloria Steinem's comments, partly because of her centrality within the field of feminism. To recall, she stated: "Never again is anyone going to say 'post-feminist' or 'post-racist' because we now understand that there is something like a third of the country that is still locked into these old hierarchies."[34] The insertion of the word *now* is what strikes me, as it is such a clear instance of the attempt at presentism that have characterised the responses listed above. To assert that we are no longer able to say "post-racial" or "post-feminist" given the election results presumes that previously both were legitimate claims to make. Indeed most of the comments presented above allude to the idea that something has shifted; American feminists are being forced to confront something. This is a disappointment on many levels: it affects their daughters, who would have benefitted from a US female president as a role model; it suggests there are many

American women who do not hold the progressive feminist views they hold; and it shatters the myth of feminist solidarity. Most of these points revolve around gender and what this means for American feminism. Very rarely is race mentioned, despite the fact that what is shocking is that it is white women who voted for Trump in large numbers, not *women*, not *working-class women*, and not *women who do not identify as liberal*. Reading the comments above, one might think that gender was the important category to focus on in trying to decipher the election results. Instead, I argue that race should be understood as the *master category*, a category that emerges from scholarship on intersectionality.

This ties in with broader support for Hillary Clinton by American feminists even at the earlier stages where she was up against Bernie Sanders in the race for Democratic Party nominee. This support was justified with claims about having a "strong female role model" for young American woman, without interrogating which young women would identify with Hillary Clinton. This support for Clinton over Sanders—an avid supporter of social justice whose policies would have likely changed the lives of many working-class women of colour in the US—suggests once again the primacy of gender over race, class, sexuality, and so on. To argue that Clinton is a good role model for women ignores her role in promoting both imperial and domestic violence against people of colour, including women, and her track record as a supporter of harsh neoliberal policies that have had the worst effects on marginalised women. One is left asking: Which women would Clinton have been a good role model for?

Intersectionality has emerged as one of the most important interventions in feminist theory and activism over the past few decades. Based on the premise that social categories are not neatly separable in our daily lived experiences, our analysis of these experiences should also not fall into distinct categorisations. Rather, we should look at the ways in which categories intersect with one another to create very particular effects. Kimberle Crenshaw, who coined the concept, made this argument based on her experience in courtrooms and with the law, which had trouble accounting for the fact that Black women experienced oppression on different fronts.[35] This has very quickly become a prominent feature of gender analysis in the academy today, as well as activism and broader social movement organising across the globe. While on the one hand, this diffusion has led to a de-radicalisation of the concept itself; on the other hand, it signals the need to de-centre gender and bring other social categories to the forefront of our work.

I want to bring in Dubravka Zarkov's concept of a master category to further probe some of the responses of feminists to the election of Trump. The concept proposes that while the idea that different positionalities and marginalisations are always intersecting with one another to produce complex realities, in certain situations a certain category or positionality will emerge as more important than others (Zarkov in Lutz, Vivar and Supik 2011, 109). This echoes Nira Yuval-Davis's similar argument that in specific historical situations and in relation to specific people, some social divisions may emerge as more important (ibid, 160). This section argues that in the context of the 2016 US election and the many issues and demographics affected by it, the category of race should be understood as a master category that was more influential in determining the outcome of the election than other social categories. This is not to suggest that race can be understood separately from class, gender, sexuality, or other categories; rather, it is to posit that the shock many feminists felt at the election result was a direct consequence of their privileging of gender at the expense of race, and in turn a reflection of the fact that they continue to ignore racism, capitalism, empire and other structures as constitutive of the modern world order. Instead, the election and its aftermath often employed racialized logics that remind us to think of white female voters as primarily acting in support of a racial, rather than gendered, project. In other words, the master category was race, not gender. The irony is that while white female voters may have voted based on racial loyalty, Trump's project is essentially one that is both racist and patriarchal. It utilises white women's racial loyalty to expand racialized persecution, while at the same time elevating white men above white women.[36] Thus on the one hand, for the white women who voted for Trump—even considering that there are many complex reasons behind this—their protection of a racial project that privileges white women at the expense of other groups of women signifies race as a master category rather than gender. On the other hand, their protection of this racial project also works to elevate Trump's patriarchal project, thus making white women complicit in their own injury.

The privileging of race, or to be more precise a racialized system of class, gender, and nationhood, should not be seen as something new. As I have shown, this continues in a long historical trajectory whereby upholding the racialized and imperial status quo was seen as the priority over global sisterhood or justice for all women. It is this historical lineage that is important to note, given the tendency to portray this "betrayal" as something new. Gloria Wekker's writing on wilful ignorance around things we don't want to see is useful: "Culturally determined blind spots lead to [a] hierarchical, colonial division of labour: we are dealing here with a toxic heritage, the epistemic violence of a colonial discourse in which white people have silently and self-evidently assigned themselves a normative and superior position, the teleological axis or endpoint of development, and other women are always already located in relation to them."[37] It is precisely the absence of race that continues to allow liberal feminists to express shock at events such as Trump's victory. Shifting away from race and imperialism as issues people wilfully ignore to seeing them as master categories in current US politics is an important move in any intersectional analysis of gender in the contemporary Euro-American world.

To unpack the responses further, two tendencies become clear in analysing white, liberal feminist responses to the election. The first has been to blame white working-class women for the vote. Susan Faludi writes: "One of the great failures—of the many failures of our broken and barely functional Fourth Estate—was the lack of substantive reportage, much less intelligent diagnosis, on the state of mind of white working-class women. Did white working-class women betray feminism, or did feminism betray them?"[38] Her article argues that liberal feminists betrayed working-class feminists; race is barely mentioned. It is again about constructing a white, liberal progressive form of feminism and a conservative regressive one; this is a class-based division, according to Faludi, whereby liberal feminists ignored their class privileges and thus betrayed working-class women, who then went on to vote for Trump in their own act of betrayal. Nowhere in this analysis is the question of race mentioned.

The second, and related, tendency has been to see the election of Trump as a failure of "lean-in" feminism. Goldberg writes: "Before Nov. 8, it looked as if the arc of history was bending toward women. Trump's victory has obliterated this narrative. The very idea that women are equal citizens, that barriers to their full human flourishing should be identified and removed, is now up for grabs."[39] The article goes on to list all of the institutional support women are likely to lose under the Trump presidency, from *Roe v. Wade* to abortion funding. Nowhere is the category "women" disaggregated. Race is not mentioned, nor is the fact that the responsibility for Clinton's loss is not shared equally among women. For white liberal feminists, this is seen as a loss for all women. Clinton was supposed to have brought about the moment when the glass ceiling would finally be broken. Instead, their analysis of why so many white women voted for Trump centres around the idea that Clinton's *brand* of feminism was the problem. It was too elitist, too corporate, too lean-in. In other words, women voted for Trump because they disliked Clinton's form of feminism.

In a more reflective take on the election, Clio Chang writes: "There's no denying that Donald Trump's victory was a setback for women's rights. It certainly doesn't speak well of a country that it elected a man who has repeatedly humiliated women in public and has been accused multiple times of harassment and assault. But that doesn't mean that the election was a referendum on whether women could be trusted to hold power, or that women as a whole were rejected. In fact, while sexism was clearly a major factor in the election, it was only a referendum on one woman, who practiced one type of feminist politics. It marked the end of Clinton's brand of feminism—call it trickle-down feminism—and the introduction, hopefully, of a more egalitarian feminist politics to the mainstream."[40] Similarly, Clover Hope writes for Jezebel: "Overwhelmingly, white people voted to preserve whiteness. Sixty-three percent of white men voted Trump. The toughest pill is that fifty-three percent of white women followed them. Institutionally-educated and middle class white people voted to retain their power. *The truth is that this is how it's always been.* The fear is that we continue to live with the knowledge that all along, it was you" (italics my own).[41]

CONCLUSION

Using the concepts of master categories/willful ignorance, it becomes clear that through the attempts by liberal feminists to centre gender, they reproduced their historical wilful ignorance of race. In other words, despite the supposed popularity of intersectionality as a concept, liberal feminist responses in effect demonstrated an attachment to gender as a master category, when in fact, as I argue, race should be understood as the master category in this particular instance. Understanding US politics through the lens of racialized gender allows for a more productive engagement with how race, nation, gender, and imperialism have always co-constituted one another across the globe.

This chapter has also argued that white, liberal feminists continue to be inattentive to questions of race and imperialism. Through expressing shock at the election results, the feminists quoted in this chapter demonstrate a detachment from the ways in which race and gender constitute one another in the American imaginary. An awareness of historical legacies, as well as current political currents, may have enlightened these feminists as to the role race and racism plays in US nation-building. Instead, many deployed *white innocence*, demonstrated through their shock and anguish. This innocence is not, however, defensible—indeed, it is not even innocent. To remain innocent means to remain ignorant; and this is a wilful, active process, not an accidental passive one.

White innocence continues to be a very real barrier to solidarity between and among women, both inside nations as well as at the global level. If Sojourner Truth was with us today, it is likely she would still ask the same question: Ain't I a woman? If Huda Sha'arawi and Nabawiya Moussa were with us, would they find that there is still a deafening silence on the part of US and European liberal feminists on the question of Palestine—despite the fact that the occupation of Palestinian territory has expanded? The election of Trump should have provoked anger, fear, and frustration; and for most people it did. But for some women—white, liberal, Western feminists—it also came as a shock. To other women—women of colour, women from the Global South, nonbinary women—this shock came as no surprise, it was merely a case of history repeating itself—this is, after all, how it has always been.

NOTES

1. Joan Walsh, "What I Got Wrong About Hillary Clinton—and What Other Feminists Get Wrong About Her Now," *The Nation*, November 14, 2016, https://www.thenation.com/article/what-i-got-wrong-about-hillary-clinton-and-what-other-feminists-get-wrong-about-her-now/.

2. M. Goldberg, "The Empire Strikes Back," *Slate*, December 27, 2016, https://slate.com/human-interest/2016/12/2016-was-the-year-the-feminist-bubble-burst.html.

3. Here the debate around the "white working class" is central, as it has been identified as the major factor behind Trump's victory despite evidence suggesting the white middle class was more responsible. For two excellent discussions, see: Lisa Tilley, "The Making of the 'White Working Class': Where Fascist Resurgence Meets Leftist White Anxiety," *Wildcat Dispatches*, December 05, 2016, https://wildcatdispatches.org/2016/11/28/lisa-tilley-the-making-of-the-white-working-class-where-fascist-resurgence-meets-leftist-white-anxiety/; David Roediger, "Who's Afraid of the White Working Class?: On Joan C. Williams's White Working Class: Overcoming Class Cluelessness in America," *Los Angeles Review of Books*, May 17, 2017, https://lareviewofbooks.org/article/whos-afraid-of-the-white-working-class-on-joan-c-williamss-white-working-class-overcoming-class-cluelessness-in-america/.

4. These are presented and discussed in detail further on. For a sample, see: Rebecca Traister, "Shattered," *NY Magazine,* November 14, 2016, http://nymag.com/intelligencer/2016/11/hillary-clinton-didnt-shatter-the-glass-ceiling.html?gtm=top; Kristen Bellstrom, "Gloria Steinem: After Trump's Election, the U.S. Is Like a Victim of Domestic Abuse," *Fortune*, November 17, 2016, https://fortune.com/2016/11/17/gloria-steinem-annie-leibovitz-trump/; Susan Chira, "Feminism Lost. Now What?" *New York Times,* December 30, 2016, https://www.nytimes.com/2016/12/30/opinion/sunday/feminism-lost-now-what.html?_r=0; Susan Faludi, "Where Is Feminism Now?" *Democracy: A Journal of Ideas*, Winter 2017, https://democracyjournal.org/magazine/43/where-is-feminism-now/; Lucy Clarke-Billings, "'Feminism Takes Massive Hit' as Donald Trump Celebrates Election Victory: Women's Group," *Newsweek,* November 9, 2016, https://www.newsweek.com/feminism-massive-hit-donald-trump-election-victory-womens-group-518899.

5. This statistic quickly became the go-to statistic on the percentage of white women who voted for Trump. See: Hannah Allam, "White Women's Support for Trump Is a Thorny Issue for Some Marchers of Color," *New Observer,* January 21, 2017, https://www.newsobserver.com/news/politics-government/article127985374.html.

6. Gloria Wekker, *White Innocence: Paradoxes of Colonialism and Race* (Durham: Duke University Press, 2016).

7. Dubravka Zarkov, "Framing Intersectionality: An Introduction," in *Framing Intersectionality*, ed. Helma Lutz et al. (London: Routledge, 2016), 15–36.

8. bell hooks, *Feminist Theory: From Margin to Center* (London: Pluto Press 2000), 164.

9. Inter alia: Chandra Mohanty, "Under Western Eyes: Feminist Scholarship and Colonial Discourses," *Feminist Review 1*, no. 30, (1988): 61–88; hooks, *Feminist Theory*; Angela Davis, *Women, Race, & Class* (New York: Vintage, 1981).

10. Sara Farris, *In the Name of Women's Rights: The Rise of Femonationalism* (Durham: Duke University Press, 2017).

11. Chandra Mohanty, *Under Western Eyes*; Anne McClintock, *Imperial Leather: Race, Gender, and Sexuality in the Colonial Contest*. (London: Routledge, 2013); Avtar Brah and Ann Phoenix, "Ain't I a Woman? Revisiting Intersectionality," *Journal of International Women's Studies* 5, no. 3, (2012): 75–86; Carole Boyce Davies, *Left of Karl Marx: The Political Life of Black Communist Claudia Jones*, (Durham: Duke University Press, 2007); Christine Bolt, *Sisterhood Questioned: Race, Class and Internationalism in the American and British Women's Movements c. 1880s–1970s*. (London: Routledge, 2004); M. Jacqui Alexander and Chandra Mohanty, *Feminist Genealogies, Colonial Legacies, Democratic Futures*. (London: Routledge, 1997); Karen Kaplan, "The Politics of Location as a Transnational Feminist Critical Practice," in *Scattered Hegemonies, Postmodernity and Transnational Feminist Practices*, ed. Inderpal Grewal (Twin Cities: University of Minnesota Press, 1994), 137–52.

12. Beth Baron, *Egypt as a Woman: Nationalism, Gender, and Politics*. (Berkeley: University of California Press, 2005), 31.

13. Beth Baron, *Egypt as a Woman*, 223.

14. Margot Badran, *Feminists, Islam, and Nation: Gender and the Making of Modern Egypt*. (Princeton: Princeton University Press, 1996), 238.

15. Margot Badran, *Feminists, Islam and Nation,* 13.

16. Gloria Wekker, *White Innocence*, 237.

17. Gloria Wekker, *White Innocence*, 220.

18. Gloria Wekker, *White Innocence*, 237.

19. Gloria Wekker, *White Innocence*, 535.

20. Sara Salem and Vanessa Eileen-Thomas, "Old Racisms, New Masks: On the Continuing Discontinuities of Racism and the Erasure of Race in European Contexts," *Nineteen Sixty Nine: An Ethnic Studies Journal*, 2016, https://escholarship.org/uc/item/98p8q169.

21. Domenico Losurdo, *Liberalism: A Counter-History*. (London: Verso, 2014).

22. Domenico Losurdo, *Liberalism.*

23. Joan Scott, *Only Paradoxes to Offer: French Feminists and the Rights of Man*. (Cambridge: Harvard University Press, 2009); Antoinette Burton, *Burdens of History: British Feminists, Indian Women, and Imperial Culture, 1865–1915*. (Chapel Hill: University of North Carolina Press, 1993); Chandra Mohanty, *Under Western Eyes*; Catherine Rottenberg, "The Rise of Neoliberal Feminism," *Cultural Studies*, *28*, no. 2, (2014): 418–37; Sara Farris, *In the Name of Women's Rights*.

24. Rebecca Traister, "Shattered."

25. Rebecca Traister, "Shattered."

26. Kristen Bellstrom, "Gloria Steinem."

27. Susan Chira, "Feminism Lost."

28. Susan Chira, "Feminism Lost."

29. Susan Chira, "Feminism Lost."

30. Susan Faludi, "Where Is Feminism Now?"

31. Lucy Clarke-Billings, "Feminism Takes Massive Hit."

32. Michelle Goldberg, "The Empire Strikes Back."

33. Joan Walsh, "What I Got Wrong About Hillary Clinton."

34. Kristen Bellstrom, "Gloria Steinem."

35. Kimberlé Crenshaw, "Mapping the Margins: Intersectionality, Identity Politics, and Violence against Women of Color," *Stanford Law Review* (1991): 1241–299.

36. A special thanks to Lisa Tilley for helping me think through this point.

37. 1368.

38. Susan Faludi, "Where Is Feminism Now?"

39. Michelle Goldberg, "The Empire Strikes Back."

40. Clio Chang, "What Is the Post-Hillary Feminism?" *New Republic*, November 22, 2016, https://newrepublic.com/article/138933/post-hillary-feminism.

41. Clover Hope, "All Along It Was You," *Jezebel*, November 9, 2016, https://theslot.jezebel.com/all-along-it-was-you-1788758934.

5

BUILDING KINFULNESS

Beth Hinderliter

At a lecture in 2017, reproduction justice scholar and activist Loretta Ross remarked that she has often felt very othered at the hands of people who have misunderstood intersectionality theory. Her words stuck with me as I've navigated conversations and exchanges (often in Women's and Gender Studies spaces) where intersectionality is often perceived as pertaining to identities, rather defined by systems and structures of power. This shallow, rhetorical engagement of intersectionality purposively distorts Kimberlé Crenshaw's original articulation of the idea, which was intended to provide a framework for understanding the simultaneity and interactions of many forms of structural oppression.[1] Reducing intersectionality to subject-centered and mutable ideas about identity not only naively erases the functioning of power, but moreover cements its current status quo firmly into place. Beyond being commonly misinterpreted, intersectionality theory is also often frequently summoned by jargon talkers, who deliberately invoke the concept as a screen mechanism to veil, rather than challenge, entrenched forms of privilege. "Yes, race is important," one feminist claimed in the course of committee work, "and as we are good at intersectionality, we can be assured that race will enter into our conversations on gender and sexuality." But it didn't. Effectively in that meeting space, intersectionality was called upon to do the opposite of its intentions, allowing the shelving of topics of race and racism pertaining to the lives of women on campus. Within women-centered spaces of the academy, there is often a self-proclaimed ownership by those who identify themselves as "women" or "feminists" who feel that adding issues of race and racism and other modalities of oppression beyond gender into their agenda waters down advocacy for women—who as a category, they argue—still haven't made it to positions of equality either in the academy or in society at large. Furthermore, when they insist on calling their approach intersectional, these feminists suppress the Black Feminist history and orientation of intersectionality.

Intersectionality is thus purposively manipulated in these spaces, where women who feel challenged by its parameters and concepts dismantle its efficacy under the guise of advocacy. This enacts divisions and enforces barriers to communication and relationship building. As Sara Ahmed has pointed out, diversity work is often most effectively blocked by simply agreeing to it, without ever acting on or putting agreed-upon resolutions and recommendations into practice. We need to look at how this happens within, not just outside of, spaces recognized as feminist spaces in our organizations and institutions. As talk of diversity supplants notions of inclusion in the academy at large, feminist spaces largely ignore that diversity is not intersectionality. It's not even anti-racism. As Audre Lorde argued in 1981 and is still true today, "Mainstream communication does not want women, particularly white women, responding to racism. It wants racism to be accepted as an immutable given in the fabric of existence, like evening time or the common cold."[2]

Walking down a hallway, outside of a class dealing with diversity issues, I pause to hear a professor espousing that cross-cultural miscommunication and incompetency happen due to differences that are below the radar of most sensitive people. Using a model of an iceberg, she explains that what is below the surface, what we don't see, causes breakdowns in understanding people with different backgrounds than us. It was meant as a feel-good moment where students were absolved of responsibility to what was labeled invisible, out of reach, unknowable, "other." It was another moment where the misunderstanding of intersectionality facilitated the "othering" of difference, rather than building accountability across difference. The professor's approach instrumentalized intersectionality as a preformatted methodology meant to be applied to discreet identities, rather than as the framework which emerges out of the constantly changing traffic on the streets of our society, as Kimberlé Crenshaw envisioned in her formulation of the concept. Such reformist neoliberal invocations of diversity absolve subjects of responsibility while dehistoricizing all forms of oppression. Diversity rhetoric in the academy is most often paired with tolerance, and tolerance is at the core of liberal reformism.

As Jasbir Puar has pointed out, seeing identity as a process or encounter that is fluid and evolving lets us see intersectionality as "a much more porous paradigm than the standardization of method inherent to a discipline has allowed it to be; the institutionalization of women's studies in the U.S. has led to demands for a subject/s (subject X, in fact) and a method."[3] To put it another way, a lot of academic feminism studies the language of intersectionality, only in order to replicate it in the right context without doing the emotional work or building the needed lived relationships to turn that language into more than just hollow words. As jargon talkers rather than critical thinkers, they end up doing the work of post-slavery imperialism itself. Brittney Cooper calls us out: what happens "if we get all of the academic tenets of feminism right, if we get our intersectionality right, and we name all our identities properly and we have this sort of vain intersectional analysis—but you treat people like shit—you don't really love yourself, or other women, or femme or queer folk, or trans folk. If you don't really love and are not really committed to being in struggle in ways that help everybody to live better, and live more fully, then you're not doing shit."[4]

Solidarity is often posited within diversity work rather than enacted; as if solidarity was the work of the 1970s and now that we are all properly intersectional that work can be dispensed with. Rather, that work is always only just starting. By its nature, the work of building solidarity must be done, redone, examined, built, rebuilt and reframed for a continued existence. "Solidarity across differences is not a pre-existing condition," Ruha Benjamin reminds us, "but an outgrowth generated in the day-to-day labor of building political movements. Reorienting ourselves towards kinship not as a precursor but as an effect of social struggle denaturalizes what kinfulness means and how to enact it."[5] Benjamin's deliberate use of the term *kinship* is carefully poised to challenge assumptions that plague current mainstream feminism. Kinfulness rejects the logic of sorting, classifying, and defining relations according to nationalism, ethnocentrism, or capitalist property laws. Drawing on Donna Haraway's use of the term *kin* as a framework for a multispecies environmental justice that denies human exceptionalism,

Benjamin calls attention to kinfulness as critical for building capacities and relationships that are nurturing, creative, impactful and which persist into a transformative future. As Christina Sharpe points out, the laws of U.S. chattel slavery and Jim Crow which historically defined white kinship (legally, familially, and politically) also refused to recognize Black personhood. "They make and unmake persons and families," Sharpe writes, "and assign human beings value in and of themselves, or not."[6] White-identified people are compelled to lose their kin formed under these domineering logics and forge a solidaritous kinfulness in its place. To that end, Deborah Gabriel's term "frequent ally-occasional enemy" is effective in revealing the fractional, shifting and often duplicitous nature of relationships across difference.[7] These "frequent allies-occasional enemies" discriminate at whim, withholding expected support at often the most critical moments.

Learning from the failures of allyship is a critical building block for collective activism and resistance. Cooper's hashtag #goaskawhitefeminist—which directs those who are tired of having to explain racism and its effects to shift the burden elsewhere—compellingly foregrounds racialized encounters with such "frequent ally-occasional enemies." White feminists are called on to check their own racial privilege, to speak out against racism in conversations with other white folk, and to call attention to those moments where the solidarity of whiteness solicits frequent allies to become those occasional enemies. Cooper asks white feminists to build kinship in these moments of exchange on social media, suggesting that white feminists should "go get your people."

This exhortation to "go get your people" spoke to me as an educator as white people have historically rejected cohesive group identity, while nonetheless conjuring it into being and profiting from its existence. Offering this in conversation with a friend, she pointed out to me that she never gets to escape raced communal responsibility. Her comment reminded me of the danger of fantasies of kinship (that are not unrealized because never constructed, becoming the stuff of interracial fetishes and imaginary machinations) as well as of fantasies of non-kinship ("I am not *those* white people") that include privileged performances of difference within sameness from dominant social positions and privilege.

I recalled a dinner I had shared with a white female colleague who complained to me how she didn't have time or energy for anyone who didn't hold her same political opinions. She recounted how she—like so many others I knew—had gone on a "unfriending" spree on Facebook during and after the presidential election in 2016. Despite what ties or histories may have originally brought them together as FB friends, she pruned out any one who supported Trump, rather than engaging them about their choices and opinions. How might a chain effect of "getting your people" make a direct impact when done with care, caution and meaningful engagement? During that conversation, I thought about entrenchment of progressive credentials—wondering who were the white people Brittney Cooper suggested I go and get. Was it the seemingly hate-filled Trump supporters, or was it those who turned their backs on others after classifying them as lost causes, a basket of deplorables? What privilege did it take to nonchalantly prune your social circles in that way? Social circles are, as Leah Lakshmi Piepzna-Samarasinha details, communities of care that facilitate the day-to-day survival of those made precarious in our current society. "No institutions exist to help us survive," she writes, "we survive because of each other. Your life is maintained by a complex, non-monetary economy of shared, reciprocal care."[8] The privilege at the heart of this pruning is a version of white guilt, that seeks to contain racism as "over there" in those "bad" white people, reducing personal implication in their behavior, limiting their contagion.

In the face of this pruning that comes with each click of the "unfriend" button on Facebook or elsewhere in face-to-face encounters, can we find ways of unpacking what is shared while troubling what is presumed in order to build kinship? What I see on a daily basis in Women and Gender Studies classes is a paralyzing fear on the part of white students of being called out as racist and elitist. Many academic spaces allow for and perpetutate this fear rather than building an environment that is sufficiently critical of majoritarianism and domination, where being called out would be both expected and appreciated. This holds many students back from creating real, rather than imagined, kinship—and it keeps feminism shallow and academic, rather than engaging our messy, emotional, and complex lives. After the 2016 election, I approached my classes with the words of Brittney Cooper ringing in my ears—that "white women should go and get your people." As I asked mostly white students to be accountable in their kinship practices, I worried about the danger of focusing on the psychology of recalcitrant white people, rather than engaging in a productive sociological analysis of race. I hoped, though, to unpack the dynamics of what some in Women's Studies had begun to refer to as the "Trump bump"—a new sense of engagement with feminism by students who now increasingly found their way into Women's Studies classes. Moreover, I wanted to know how feminism—now profiting from this Trump bump—holds its adherents' feet to the fire with the knowledge that white women voters had voted in a majority to elect Trump? Has Women's Studies been failing its students as the shelving of intersectional work enables the sanitizing of racist core beliefs?

As my class struggled to come to terms with the failed intersectionality of the Women's March on Washington, we engaged in studying both the Me Too movement in relation to the Black Lives Matter movement in order to pick apart how violence in the US is dichotomously gendered or racialized—with mainstream perceptions that the victims of gender-based violence are white women and the victims of racialized violence are black men. How do Women's Studies departments continue to perpetuate the same exclusive thinking and not advance a more radical position on dismantling power, privilege and prestige? Alice Ginsberg, editor of *The Evolution of American Women's Studies: Reflections on Triumphs, Controversies and Change* notes that Women's Studies has felt the need to "destabilize gender at the same time we insist that historically and politically a category or class of individuals called women have been systematically oppressed."[9] Lamenting that this is a tricky position to be in, Ginsburg points to a perceived problem in Women's Studies that the more it destabilizes gender, the more it dissolves its core subject: women. Yet is this not precisely the kind of challenging that Women's Studies needs—that we don't presume the category of women, womanliness and femininity as some a priori category—but rather that we start from this dissolution to grow the kinship that we need.

The fragility of mainstream feminism made apparent (not just) in the wake of Hillary Clinton's electoral defeat came from its presumption of similarity, presumptions of shared indigent response to attacks on white middle-class identity. As Sarah Ahmed has written, the neoliberal feminism advanced by Hillary Clinton or Sheryl Sanders in her book *Lean In Together* repackages feminism as "upward mobility for some women, those who accept responsibilities for their 'own well-being and self-care,' a way some women thus distance themselves from others."[10] The togetherness crafted in this version of feminism is based on a purposive exclusion of the most vulnerable in our society, which is disavowed in order to claim an inherent fragility to the white middle-class femininity that seeks advancement. In this way, white fragility is like the "beautiful soul" that Hegel described in *Phenomenology of Spirit* as morally sensitive, but incapable of action, preferring instead to sit in judgment of the inevitable shortcomings of others.

If kinship is to be enacted, crafted, and cared for—not presumed and espoused but ultimately neglected, what pedagogical strategy can best accommodate this when so much of the "Trump bump" phenomenon is based on a knee-jerk grasping of the idea of woman as category? A recent example of effective kinship building (or co-conspiracy—to use a term that another chapter in this book advocates) is a letter published after democratic politician Nancy Pelosi (and later Charles Schumer) criticized African American congresswoman Maxine Waters in June 2018. Written by self-declared white feminists to Nancy Pelosi (her staff said Pelosi read it) sought to "call in" Pelosi for what they saw as her racist and deeply problematic criticism of Waters. Waters had challenged rally attendees on June 25, 2018, to disrupt the Trump establishment by confronting cabinet members when they are seen in public at places like gas stations or restaurants. "If you see anybody from that Cabinet," Waters had said, "in a restaurant, in a department store, at a gasoline station, you get out and you create a crowd. And you push back on them. And you tell them they're not welcome anymore, anywhere." Her comment had followed on Sarah Huckabee Sanders being asked to leave a restaurant in Lexington, Virginia, by its owner earlier that June, an episode which raised public questions about issues of civility and free speech. Huckabee Sanders's father, former presidential nominee Mike Huckabee, had chimed in after this episode, declaring that bigotry was "on the menu" of that restaurant, as well as a "hate plate." Pelosi's comment sought to reject this association—made by Huckabee, Trump and others—that tagged Democrats with the hate and incivility normally seen as characteristic of Republicans instead.

Pelosi's tweet from June 25 proclaimed that "Trump's daily lack of civility has provoked responses that are predictable but unacceptable." Yet many responders on Twitter began to reject Pelosi's call for civility, celebrating the idea of ejecting Trump officials from public places in order to have "fascist free dinners." Others asked what was the difference between the refusal to serve Sanders and the "hate plate" that she serves every day to them in her role as media secretary? The letter which sought to call-in Pelosi and model intersectional white feminist allyship in support of black feminist action and speech was eventually signed by over six thousand supporters. "Writing Black women's words off as divisive," the letter's authors argued, "is not merely condescending—it echoes racist tropes that have been used for centuries to dehumanize Black people and support the structures that maintain discrimination."[11] Worse, the letter maintained, was that Pelosi's chastising condoned, if not created, unsafe conditions for Waters, who has since faced serious and escalating death threats.

Rather than call attention to a psychology of whiteness, the authors delved into the social parameters of whiteness and its blindspots (willed or unconscious). "To our great discredit," the authors of the letter announced, "white women continue to act far too often in ways that support white supremacy, even when it is to our detriment. Time and time again, we have seen women of color show up to the polls to support progressive politics, while white women cling to the regressive, and often racist, politics and politicians who long for yesteryear."[12] Their statement recalled a comment that a student had made on an exam that "black Women are literally saving our asses." This student had come though the class having made many pronouncements on the successes of the Women's March in Washington, D.C. She was from the Northern Virginia area and was emotionally invested in the March's legacy. Despite readings and conversations in the class which criticized the March's lack of intersectionality, she clung to a belief that one of the many successes of the March was its diversity. And her comment on the exam revealed the extent to which she (but also others in the class) was beholden to a neo-liberal vision of diversity—which quarantines difference as "other," renders it exotic and superhuman, while mainstreaming the majoritarian status quo as good-willed, but brittle, unchanging, and desperately fragile.

Over the course of the semester, the class revealed a profound discomfort on topics of race on the part of many students, so much so that there was a palpable sense of relief when the course began a sequence on queer theory. Those who had struggled in conversations around race rushed to show their progressive attitudes regarding LBGT+ issues. How do you convince a population that seems confident of its progressive credentials that it has work to do around its own whiteness, rather than participate in the feel-good diversity rhetoric, often apparent on higher education campuses, that sets its agenda as a mild appreciation of otherness?

Effective co-conspiracy must erase this mythological pairing of black superhuman strength in opposition to white fragility. Its toxicity was pointed out as the Twittersphere erupted with protests that black women are not here to "save people" after a public protest carried out by Therese Patricia Okoumou on July 4, 2018. Scaling the Statue of Liberty, Okoumou called attention to current inhumane ICE policies of separating immigrant children from their parents while in detention. Responding to a tweet that called Okoumou and other black women "superheroes," @teresamstout argued that "if Black women are gonna save us all the least y'all could do is listen to us say that we'd like to be acknowledged w/o using a trope. At the very least reckon that the road to your conclusions require traversing the bridges called our backs."[13] Bree Newsome, the antiracist activist who previously climbed a flag pole to remove a Confederate flag in Columbia, SC, added that "BW [Black Women] are on frontline of revolution in America & have been for generations b/c the system of white capitalist patriarchy was literally organized around our enslavement. This is also why we represent base of progressive mvmt. Y'all erase this reality thinking we exist to save others."[14]

This conversation calls on white allyship to rethink dangerous presuppositions: that black activists' words and actions are not here to "save" white people from themselves, especially those white women whose racism took precedence over their gender equality commitments in the 2016 presidential election. To dismantle white supremacist mythologizing in thought and action requires careful construction of alliances and connections via deliberate actions of co-conspiracy. Yet since the 2016 election, these kinds of alliances are increasingly threatened by a widescale public fear that any discussion of race and racism, or even of inclusion and civility, would push away rural white voters who feel alienated and frustrated with rising unemployment and poverty levels.[15] Yet as the November 2018 elections revealed, the most successful candidates to challenge "red" districts that aligned with Trump in 2016 were those who explicitly embraced a progressive agenda and were able to forge cross-racial alliances. Much work remains in building white alliances across urban to rural divides and across educational and class demographics. The election results from the 2018 Georgia gubernatorial race reveal advances made by white women embracing sisterhood with women of color since 2016: exit polls showed that Stacy Abrams gained 9 percentage points amongst white college-educated women's votes when compared to the same population who voted for Trump in the 2016 presidential election.

How can we craft the kinship we need, starting on a small scale within our classrooms? First of all, we must recognize that if our feminism is academic, it will replicate all of the oppressions inherent within the academy. White-identified people must push past fragility and brittleness to build the kinships needed for our common future. By working from the presumption that kinship must be enacted, not presupposed, and formulating power as "power with" rather than "power over," we will open ourselves to real change. This capacity to build kinship in multiplicitous, intersectional and varied forms will allow us to create the real coalitions we need that are numbering, not in the thousands, but in the millions.

NOTES

1. Kimberlé Crenshaw, "Mapping the Margins: Intersectionality, Identity Politics, and Violence Against Women of Color." *Stanford Law Review, 43* (1991): 1241–99.

2. Audre Lorde, "The Uses of Anger," *Women's Studies Quarterly,* 25, no. 1/2, Looking Back, Moving Forward: 25 Years of Women's Studies History (Spring–Summer 1997): 281.

3. Jasbir Puar, "I'd Rather Be a Cyborg Than a Goddess: Intersectionality, Assemblage, and Affective Politics," *Transversal Texts*, http://eipcp.net/transversal/0811/puar/en, Accessed on September 5, 2018.

4. Brittney Cooper as quoted in Maiysha Kai, "Eloquent Rage: Brittney Cooper Knows the Beauty of the 'Angry Black Woman,'" *The Root* (March 20, 2018), https://theglowup.theroot.com/eloquent-rage-brittney-cooper-knows-the-beauty-of-the-1823684559/amp, accessed November 3, 2018.

5. Ruha Benjamin, "Black AfterLives Matter: Cultivating Kinfulness as Reproductive Justice," *Boston Review: A Political and Literary Forum*, https://bostonreview.net/race/ruha-benjamin-black-afterlives-matter, accessed August 3, 2018. This is a version of the chapter which appeared in *Making Kin not Population: Reconceiving Generations*, eds. Clarke and Haraway. (Chicago: Prickly Paradigm Press, 2018).

6. Christina Sharpe, "Lose Your Kin," *The New Inquiry* (November 16, 2016), https://thenewinquiry.com/lose-your-kin/, accessed November 15, 2018.

7. Deborah Gabriel,. "Social Closure, White Male Privilege and Female Complicity: Why Gender Equality Still Has a Long Way to Go," http://deborahgabriel.com/2018/10/28/social-closure-white-male-privilege-and-female-complicity-why-gender-equality-still-has-a-long-way-to-go/, accessed November 5, 2018. See also Deborah Gabriel, "Collective Activism inside the Ivory Tower: Developing a Political Mission for Women of Colour in British Academia," *Political Studies Review*. Special Issue on Gender and the Profession (2019).

8. Leah Lakshmi Piepzna-Samarasinha, "A Modest Proposal for a Fair Trade Emotional Labor Economy (Centered by Disabled, Femme of Color, Working Class/Poor Genius)," *Bitch Magazine*, https://www.bitchmedia.org/article/modest-proposal-fair-trade-emotional-labor-economy/centered-disabled-femme-color-working, accessed September 24, 2018.

9. Ginsberg as quoted in Jaschik, "The Evolution of American Women's Studies," *Inside Higher Education*, March 27, 2009, https://www.insidehighered.com/news/2009/03/27/women, accessed 1/24/2017.

10. Sarah Ahmed, "Self Care as Warfare," https://feministkilljoys.com/2014/08/25/selfcare-as-warfare/, accessed Februrary 16, 2017. See also Catherine Rottenberg, "The Rise of Neoliberal Feminism," *Cultural Studies* (2013). http://www.bgu.ac.il/~rottenbe/The%20rise%20of%20neoliberal%20feminism.pdf.

11. "Calling in Nancy Pelosi," https://callinginnancypelosi.wordpress.com/open-letter-to-nancy-pelosi/, accessed July 12, 2018.

12. Ibid. https://callinginnancypelosi.wordpress.com/open-letter-to-nancy-pelosi/. Accessed July 12, 2018.

13. Kenrya Rankin, "Black Women: We're Not Superheroes, We're Human," *Colorlines*, (July 6, 2018), https://www.colorlines.com/articles/black-women-were-not-superheroes-were-human, accessed August 16, 2018.

14. Bree Newsome on Twitter, https://twitter.com/BreeNewsome/status/1014989511623880706?ref_src=twsrc%5Etfw%7Ctwcamp%5Etweetembed%7Ctwterm%5E1014989511623880706&ref_url=https%3A%2F%2Fwww.colorlines.com%2Farticles%2Fblack-women-were-not-superheroes-were-human.

15. Much in the media after the 2016 election had adhered to the standard white supremacist trope that to raise the issue of racism at all is racism itself. For example, Conor Friedersdorf in *The Atlantic* argued that calling out racism is counterproductive. "Among other problems with wielding stigma," Friedersdorf argued, "it doesn't work," https://www.theatlantic.com/politics/archive/2016/11/the-scourge-of-the-left-too-much-stigma-not-enough-persuasion/508961/. Similarly, Drake Baer claimed in *NY Magazine* that calling out white-identified people as racists plainly threatens to stifle constructive debate because of knee-jerk reactions to being labeled that way. Baer, "Language Matters If You're Trying to Persuade a Trump Voter," *The Cut* (November 2016), https://www.thecut.com/2016/11/calling-someone-racist-wont-help-your-arguement.html?mid=twitter_nymag.

6

EDUCATIONAL TRAJECTORIES OF THE FEMALE TRANS STUDENTS OF THE MOCHA CELIS SECONDARY SCHOOL IN ARGENTINA

Pablo Scharagrodsky and Magalí Pérez Riedel

Historically, transgender people have been excluded from formal educational spheres. It is not rare to find out that they hardly ever finish primary or secondary school due to structural reasons that are linked to their gender identity. Thus, discrimination by the peers and by family members and the lack of support from adults altogether lead transgender students to drop out of school and seek jobs that require no qualification. Not only does this have a negative impact on their long-term socioeconomic status, but it has concrete implications on their immediate living conditions. In Argentina alone, transgender women tend to live less than forty years, so there is an urgent need to look for ways to counter discrimination and endangerment to improve their place in power disputes on their daily lives.

For such purpose, we take our first steps in that direction in this chapter, where we approach the Mocha Celis secondary school for adults, the first one of its kind to develop an inclusive educational program for transgender people in Argentina—and in Latin America as well. We conducted focus groups and interviews with professors and principals of this high school so as to learn about the characteristics of the lives of transgender students in the past and present. Additionally, we conducted a number of interviews with female transgender students from this high school to inquire about their own educational trajectories and their views on education.

Our research employs a feminist and queer perspective to study the fields of communication and education. This theoretical framework comes as an asset to understand the inclusive educational project that members of the Mocha Celis sustain on a daily basis and the power struggles of transgender people today. To analyze our data, we utilized a qualitative methodological strategy. The research questions were as follows: A) How would the transgender students of the Mocha Celis secondary school describe their educational trajectories? B) What are their views on education today?

We found that in part transgender women were excluded from formal educational systems for adults' aversion towards their sex-gender dissidence, although there were also resistances and counter-hegemonic practices where they quit school by their own means to rebel or just to work. Some of them dropped out of school during primary school while others left during high school. They now see that going back to school is a way to find better jobs to improve their socioeconomic condition, and they feel really satisfied with having the possibility to attend the Mocha Celis School.

In the last fifteen years in Latin America, legislation and policies on sexuality and gender identities had great visibility and significant political recognition. Argentina wasn't the exception, as proven by the approval of a vast variety of bills regarding comprehensive sex education, reproductive health, the right to gender identity and equal marriage, among other topics.[1] The Comprehensive Sex Education (CSE) bill, sanctioned by Law 26150/2006, was key to building a more inclusive and democratic vision of sexuality based on the expansion and recognition of human rights. This bill was meant to create a systematic space for teaching and learning that would promote knowledge and skills for making conscious and critical decisions about the care of one's body, interpersonal relationships, the exercise of sexuality and the protection and enjoyment of children's rights.

In the last decades, there has been a slow process of criticism and fight against the patriarchal and heteronormative order.[2, 3, 4] The hierarchical and more traditional order of genders began to erode and to be put into question thanks to the emergence of new actors, imaginaries and social and political movements such as feminist and queer groups and thanks to a somewhat "receptive" political climate at that time. The fields of pedagogy and education were not exempt from this complex and contradictory process. In Argentina, as well as in several Latin American and European countries, the rights of vulnerable groups started to be recognized, such as the ones of the transgender population. In this context, in 2011, the first Latin American secondary school for trans people was born, being one of the first of its kind in the world: its name is the Mocha Celis School. Setting up this education institution covered a void that the CSE bill itself failed to cover at the time since it does not have any articles specially designed to talk about trans identities. But it was the work of the LGBTIQ[5] groups of the country (and especially those of Buenos Aires) which helped to install the agenda of this group, disseminate their legal and political claims and address the need to create learning spaces that differed from the traditionally stigmatizing ones. Having said that, this chapter sheds light on the characteristics of the educational trajectories of transgender and *travesti* women based on their past schooling experiences and on their transit through one of the first secondary schools that acknowledges and defends their right to education and to live a dignified life. Ultimately, this research shows why a critical (feminist and queer) perspective ought to be part of this and of other innovative, disruptive and disobedient proposals on education.

THEORETICAL FRAMEWORK

Recent research focuses on the living conditions of the *travesti* population and trans people as a whole.[6] On one hand, we found the book *La Gesta del Nombre Propio*, which was published for the first time in 2005 with Editorial de Madres de Plaza de Mayo and reissued in 2013. On the other hand, six years earlier, in 1999, the Ombudsman's Office attached to Human Rights of the Autonomous City of Buenos Aires, under the direction of Dr. Diana Maffía, had prepared the first report about the life situation of trans people in the city. Its name in English would be "Preliminary Report on the Situation of Transvestites in the City of Buenos Aires," and it was made with the help of the organization Asociación de Lucha por la Identidad Travesti y Transexual. These reports revealed figures that were worrying in terms of life and death, as it showed the trans persons' life expectancy is low. Additionally, their schooling rate is low, a problem that persists today just with small modifications.[7] But one of the central changes in the lives of the trans community was the result of mobilizations and campaigns carried out by the trans organizations in the last decade, and it occurred when the Gender Identity Bill No. 26743 was passed on May 9th, 2012. It meant a transformation for the political and the legal recognition of the identities and corporalities of the transgender collective. This law was the product of Argentine trans activism and its political alliances. The norm contemplated for the first time the right to modify the registry data to match the gender of the person, and it also guaranteed the access to a comprehensive and complementary health system that provides hormones and partial or complete surgical procedures (e.g., genital reassignment surgeries).[8] In parallel, the Equal Marriage Bill, Law No. 26618, sanctioned two years before the Gender Identity Law, also helped expand the rights of non-heterosexual people, recognizing their rights to marry and adoption.[9]

Considering the affluence of these legal, political and legislative processes, the activism of the LGBTIQ movements and the socio-political climate, the present work focuses its analysis on the educational trajectories of trans subjects comparing the political, pedagogical and sexual logics of the Mocha Celis secondary school with the logic of the schooling processes of the "traditional" education systems that were transited (at least partially) by the same trans subjects. Our research questions are: A) What are the meanings about the educational experiences of the female trans students before entering the Secondary School Mocha Celis? and B) What are the meanings about the educational experiences of the female trans students at the Mocha Celis school? We addressed these research questions from a feminist and queer perspective. Here in particular we follow the theories by Judith Butler.[10] For this author, sexual difference is never simply a function of material differences that are not somehow marked and shaped by discursive practices. In a way, the category of "sex" is, from the beginning, normative; that is what French philosopher Michel Foucault called a "regulatory ideal." In this direction, "sex" not only functions as a norm, but it is also part of a regulatory practice that creates the bodies it governs; that is, whose regulatory force manifests itself as a kind of productive power, the power to produce (demarcate, circumscribe, differentiate) the bodies that it controls. So that "sex" is a regulatory ideal whose materialization is imposed and achieved (or not) through certain highly regulated practices. In other words, "sex" is an ideal construct that inevitably materializes over time. It is not a simple reality or a static condition of a body, but a process by which regulatory norms materialize it and it achieves such materialization by the virtue of the forced reiteration of those norms. That this reiteration is necessary is a sign that materialization is never complete and that the bodies never fully comply with the norms by which their materialization is imposed.[11] According to Butler, sex and gender are cultural and historical constructs, meaning that sex has always been gender. The latter is the repeated stylization of the body, a series of repeated acts that freeze over time to produce the appearance of the substance, of a natural species of being.[12]

METHODS AND TECHNIQUES

The present investigation was carried out during the second semester of 2016 adopting a qualitative and interpretative approach based on a case study.[13] On one hand, we worked on the collection of information and references through the search, collection, organization, selection and analysis of documentary and bibliographic material of the institution under study and, on the other, we carried out semi-structured interviews as a data collection technique with the aim of recognizing and identifying the different meanings about the corporal, gender, sexual and desire regimes that circulated, were transmitted, produced, reproduced and resisted during the past and present school experiences of the trans students. More specifically, first we took into account many official and unofficial sources, including legal documents of the school, curriculum, own materials, magazine and newspaper articles referring to the institution, etc. Then, between August and September 2016, we conducted twelve interviews: five of them were made to second-year female trans students, four to teachers of the second-year and three to different authorities and spokespeople of the school. The selected sample was non-probabilistic, although our selection focused especially on female trans students who were between twenty-five and forty years old and who regularly attended the second year of the study plan (half of the training journey) and on teachers with the highest seniority in the institution. Our interviewees were inquired about the different meaning-making processes that took place in the past and present educational trajectories of the female transgender students. We understand the concept of educational trajectories as a diverse and heterogeneous set of experiences, knowledges, practices, sensibilities, emotions, senses and meanings that affect the path of the subjects in and through educational institutions. In a way, the educational trajectories combine the objective conditions (e.g., social, cultural, sexual, political, epistemic, family, institutional, etc.) and the subjective (habitus, as incorporated cultural capital)[14] and the different actions, tactics and strategies to preserve, maintain and/or improve people's positions in the educational facilities.[15]

THE FIRST TRANS SECONDARY SCHOOL IN LATIN AMERICA

The Mocha Celis secondary school for trans people arose in the Argentine capital at the end of 2011, although it started to operate in 2012. Its name represents an act of resistance and legal-political disobedience. "Mocha" was a *travesti* from the province of Tucuman, and she was unable to read or write. She used to work in the neighborhood of Bajo Flores, in the city of Buenos Aires. According to several testimonies, she was a fighter who publicly denounced abuse, violence and police brutality. She showed up dead with three shots on her body.[16] Therefore, the school's name is a tribute to the resistance against acts of violence, intimidation and personal and institutional persecution. When opening this high school, the Minister of Education of Argentina, Alberto Sileoni, stated that: "The climate that we are building is one of equality and for that we do not need mercy, but [we need] the righteousness of the State."[17] Equality and justice were two of the driving forces that the State itself (or better said, a part of it, not without internal tensions) began to vindicate, redefining new meanings about non-normative sexualities, desires and bodies, while incorporating certain groups that historically were condemned to social and, especially, educational failure. In line with this, researcher, philosopher and congresswoman of the Autonomous City of Buenos Aires, Diana Maffía, who had participated in the creation of the school, defended its existence by saying: "It is a highly inclusive mode of education and it reaches segments that are outside of formal education [systems]. The idea that it is inclusive on account of [people's] sexual identity is very important because, in all the research we carried out, one of the first consequences of transvestism is the abandonment of school."[18]

The school depends on the Directorate of Adults and Adolescents of the Ministerio de Educación (Ministry of Education) of the Autonomous City of Buenos Aires, and those who graduate do so with the title of Bachelor of Expert in Auxiliary Community Development. Most teachers are so politically and socially committed with the school that at first they all worked *pro bono* until they received funding from the State. Since it opened its doors in 2012, it had fifteen students, and the sum grew to forty-five in 2013.[19] The class that first graduated in 2014 was made up of twenty students and only nineteen in 2015. The following year, while this research was being conducted, there were a total of ninety students (forty in 1st year, twenty-five in 2nd and other twenty-five in 3rd year). However, students from past classes that had subjects pending approval came back to finish school, and then there were thirty-one new graduates by the end of 2016. But Principal Francisco Quiñones worries about the figures because usually only half of the students come to class on a regular basis: this is 50 percent of those who had enrolled. He notices that in winter the number of attendees is even lower, and adds that the dropout rate is 30 percent per year.

The format of the educational institution Mocha Celis is very particular as it has its roots in popular high schools for young people and adults, known in Argentina with the name of popular baccalaureates (*bachilleratos populares*). In part, they were constituted as alternative political-educational projects that differed and were opposed to the crystallized and, in many ways, homogenizing and unequal dominant model of the modern schooling system.[20] Although many of the popular secondary schools existed during a good part of the twentieth century, with different formats they multiplied right after the political, social and financial crisis of 2001. It should be reminded that this event hiked up the levels of social exclusion and caused a significant increase of the levels of social vulnerability of broad sectors of the population as it had never happened before in Argentine history.

Thanks to the mobilization and political commitment of different social actors (labor unions, social organizations, educators' cooperatives, movements of unemployed people, etc.), popular high schools for young people and adults were constituted, expanded and consolidated after 2001. According to social anthropologist and researcher Marina Ampudia, the period between 2007 and 2012 represented the moment of the greatest expansion of popular baccalaureates in Argentina.[21] In 2007, there were sixteen, and by the end of 2011, there were more than seventy. An official report published by the Ministerio of Educación y Deporte (Ministry of Education and Sports) in 2016 showed that there were eighty-six popular high schools in the country, although most of them were concentrated in the Metropolitan Area of Buenos Aires: 39.5 percent were in the Autonomous City of Buenos Aires, 56 percent in its surroundings, and the remaining 4.5 percent were spread in provinces like Santa Fe and Mendoza.[22] Another report from 2015 shows that most of these popular high schools (67.4 percent) are set up in popular neighborhoods, while 17.4 percent are located in city centers and the remaining 15.2 percent are in settlements and shanty towns (*villas*). However, it must be pointed out that not all of them are authorized to issue official high school diplomas: only 45 percent (thirty-nine out of eighty-six) count with the State's official recognition. This makes up a total of twenty-three schools in the capital city, fourteen in the Province of Buenos Aires and only two in the rest of the country.[23]

In general, these popular schools were conceptually influenced by critical theories (especially Freirean pedagogy) and, in part, by post-critical theories on education.[24] They usually came from self-managed, cooperative and community backgrounds, and they aimed to educate free-thinkers and political subjects to have a critical view about capitalism, neoliberalism, the growing commodification of social life and modern patriarchy.[25] Moreover, they rebuilt the teacher-student-knowledge relationship and the authority-power dyad by proposing pedagogical relationships that were more egalitarian, interactive, empathetic and participatory, and that had a strong political and social commitment. They redefined the main pedagogical conceptions, and they modified traditional ideas about the curriculum, the didactics and the organization of the institution, the evaluation and the teaching and learning processes by defending the prominence and self-management of the very own teachers and, especially, the voice and authority of students. In other words, these baccalaureates stood behind the idea that the dialogical pedagogical processes between educators and learners consisted of an exchange of diverse types of knowledge in a relationship without hierarchies; they also propounded the establishment of pedagogical pairs or teaching teams in every subject and field; a curriculum that combined the official guidelines with a pedagogical proposal collectively built in each school; the creation of rules of coexistence made by teachers and students; alternative forms of qualitative evaluation that focused on the processes of education rather than on quantitative grades that measure the learning of basic contents; a pedagogical approach that questioned the status quo with the aim of forming critical students; a pedagogical perspective oriented towards social change; permanent spaces for (self) training in popular education and (self) reflection of the teaching and pedagogical practices of popular secondary schools.[26] Over time, these spaces did not turn into something homogeneous as they presented political and managerial differences. Yet these education devices somehow redefined the relationships between the State, the civil society and the public sphere. Of course, this change included social actors that had been historically excluded from the education system, as it now allowed to build more horizontal, democratic and fair relationships of power and authority. One way or the other, with their multiple and diverse political strategies, most of the popular schools had a counter-hegemonic stand against the prevailing socio-political order, and they took action through anti-capitalist practices, a libertarian pedagogy and an empowering and emancipating political role, and with the social commitment of sub-alternized groups.

In this context, it is possible to affirm that the Mocha Celis public school tried to respond to the demand for inclusion in the Argentine education system, focusing (not exclusively) in the reception of transgender people who were over sixteen years old. As stated above, this group has historically been stigmatized and set aside from the formal educational institutions due to more implicit or explicit, material or symbolic, discriminatory practices. The few investigations on the trans collective in Argentina indicate that, on average, they live for only thirty-five years, that 80 percent of them are sex workers, and that only 20 percent have access to secondary school.[27, 28] Having said that, the Mocha Celis School aims to reverse this unfair situation by training transgender people to enable them to improve their living and working conditions so they can have further employment and career opportunities. It also seeks to promote the empowerment of trans people through the creation of self-managed work cooperatives to lower their involvement in sex work and to put an end to the abandonment and violence that they face.[29]

The school's curriculum is actually driven by these goals, as seen in the lessons that make up the three academic years. The subjects are divided into four large areas: natural sciences, communication and language, social sciences and vocational courses. They all address social, health, sexual and community problems. A lesson that stands out among the rest is education and gender, although it should be said that the gender perspective is in the core of all of them. As professor Agustín Fuchs claims, there is a clear critical social and gender perspective in the school.[30] Another professor claims that the school wasn't thought as an exclusionary institution but rather as a space that includes diversity as a whole: it is a space free of discrimination, free of sexism, free of stigmatization. She acknowledges that "it's been said that this is a school for '*travesti* girls,' but we say it's a lot more; first, because trans identities are not just '*travesti* girls,' there are trans men, transgender women, transsexuals, there are very different ways to name and perceive oneself."[31] In fact, statistically speaking, only 40 percent of the students of 2016 were not cisgender, while the rest is made up of sexually and socially subaltern groups: Afro and indigenous descendants, inhabitants of settlements and shanty towns and more people with diverse identities.

But as we said before, the gender perspective here is key. As a matter of fact, Principal Quiñones quotes Butler in some of our meetings, showing the influence of queer theories in their educational practices questioning the norm, the processes of normalization and the hegemonic imaginary that portray most of his students as abject beings because of their gender, sexual orientation, race/ethnicity, shape, size, nationality, (dis)ability, age, health, employment status and SES, to name a few. Latin American and Argentine approaches to feminist and queer theories are influenced both by regional and transnational processes. Affected by years of military dictatorships, cycles of political crises, economic recession, police repression and other forms of institutional violence, the emergence and development of local queer theories and activism argue for a social and cultural change that would bring respect to sub-alternized groups while they aim to challenge and overturn all forms of material and symbolic oppression.[32] However, this intersectional and queer approach to education was not common in other institutions. According to Fuchs, "In the public school there is no debate, for example, on the issue of the use of bathrooms, separate gymnastics, etc. Everything is taught from a hetero-normative and binary perspective."[33] In this context, we ask ourselves about the meanings that the members of this school (teachers, authorities and female trans students) assign to bodies, desires and sexualities as we inquire about the educational trajectories and the different meanings that trans students have about the educational systems that they attended during their lives, in the past and in the present.

THE TRANS SCHOOL EXPERIENCE BEFORE ENTERING THE MOCHA CELIS SCHOOL

All of the interviewees agree that their experiences at school were marked by the realization of their own transgender identities. The more they drifted away from what was "normal," the more they would get bullied by classmates or punished by principals and professors. They all point out that there were gendered divisions in many spaces and activities at school: boys and girls had to form different lines, practice different sports and go to separate bathrooms. Those who distanced themselves from the normative social expectations and representations on normative genders and sexualities then started to face different forms of backlash, which in some cases even lead them to quit school. Our interviewees claim that professors at the time lacked a gender perspective, and that schools have never been keen on trans identities. A recurrent idea was that schools were hostile and not welcoming towards trans people. As reported in a previous study, one *travesti* student found that: "One left high school because you were called by your male name or your appearance was different, or you decided that your life would be different from the others. So for me, that's it. Now we are much more included in society and not before. Why would you study if in the street no one will ask you for a degree? High heels and make up, and that's it!"[34]

Participant A, who is now a trans activist and mother of a child, dropped out of high school ten years ago. She remembers suffering bullying from her peers. She would stand up for herself by punching them back, but then she would get blamed and punished for that—her bullies wouldn't. She stopped going to school because of the discrimination she faced. Participant B had a similar experience during her childhood. She was eleven years old when she quit primary school, more than twenty years ago. Her professors and principals accused her of being a "deviant" and a homosexual. She feels she was kicked out of that institution because the principal had told her mother to send her to a psychologist and return only if she had a certificate stating she was fine. But her mother had never sent her to the therapist and therefore she couldn't go back to class. She believes that the State is in debt with her for all the time she lost. She adds that this is what many trans women went through in their childhood and youth.

Nevertheless, their schooling processes were not only affected by the discrimination from school members and peers; they were also affected by family issues and, specifically, by socioeconomic factors. It wasn't uncommon to hear our interviewees say that they weren't accepted at home, so they had to move out, but they couldn't find stable jobs and had to choose work over school. Participant C is now a housekeeper. She assisted at a boarding school over thirty years ago. She believes her professors weren't aware of topics such as discrimination and acceptance of the other like they are now. So when she refused to engage in activities with boys, such as playing soccer, she would be punished by having to kneel under the sun on top of a bunch of corn. However, discrimination was not the reason why she dropped out of school. When she left from her parents' house, she had to work for survival. And even though she tried to go back to school, her working conditions were so poor that she was unable to work and study at the same time. She points out that all the jobs a trans woman could choose from were housekeeping or prostitution.

The family and the socioeconomic struggles and the boys/girl division at school appeared in most of the narratives of the trans students we talked to. Some even had lots of things in common with the past experiences of their teachers that are also transgender women. Professor E provided her insights about her female trans students. She sees that most of them had to quit studying to work as prostitutes. She argues they haven't gone back to school because they were scared they would be rejected again. Trans professor F agrees with the fact that Argentine's education system is patriarchal and cisheteronormative. As stated above, traditional educational institutions reproduce a matrix of thought that condenses gendered hierarchies and perpetuates a grid of intelligibility that excludes transgender identities, bodies and desires. What is more, they put boundaries on who can have access to formal education by denying the right to education and to a life free of discrimination to those who do not conform to the set of explicit or implicit traditional gendered rules. They can also perpetrate discrimination and institutional violence against people with non-normative genders through different forms of punishment, such as blaming a person who stood up for herself when being harassed, or accusing another student of being psychologically unstable by calling her a homosexual deviant and by obliging her to go to therapy, making evident some moral and medical discourses that pathologize and discriminate trans identities. If we add these factors to the low-SES background of our interviewees, it sheds light on the reasons why they dropped out of school and why the Mocha Celis high school intends to overturn those issues.

THE TRANS SCHOOL EXPERIENCE IN THE MOCHA CELIS SCHOOL

Those who make up the Mocha Celis popular baccalaureate are conscious of the differences between their institute and the traditional ones. They acknowledge that this new space reacts against cisgender norms—the most evident proof is the school's logo, which has the face of the Argentine "Father of Education" Domingo Faustino Sarmiento, with dyed hair and red lipstick. But it also allows the coexistence of different people in a positive environment, promoting relationships that are based on principles of equality and respect and where the participants are aware of their role as actors for social change.

All our interviewees say that this school represents an act of resistance in the face of the adversities they face or had faced on a daily basis: when working on the streets, when expressing their genders as they are, when attending school, when simply being themselves. In that way, they have a shared feeling that the school is a refuge, a shelter, a safe place. Moreover, they claim it is their second home; there, they eat, study, learn and make friends. They say they are part of something bigger, like a family that has no bonds by blood but by choice. This can even be seen in the way that the school provides meals and study grants to help students remain in school and finish their courses. Even if they miss class for too long, students will receive a phone call from their principal as he worries students may drop out.

Students feel they belong to the school. There is a sense of belonging, a bond as a community. They take ownership of their place in it as they embrace and seize their opportunity to finish school. One of the interviewees claims that schools normally tend to be discriminatory towards trans students through actions and values that are embodied by the professors or the principals. She perceives that the Mocha Celis School is different: it is inclusive, and it is open to all identities. Moreover, as one of her teachers explains, the school is inclusive in a comprehensive way, not only because of the contents that are taught but also because of the food, the financial aid and the distinctive pedagogical approach from the popular schools.

All in all, the subjects at the Mocha Celis are just like those in any other school, but only with some changes. For example, a professor told us she once gave a lesson on math by explaining and teaching how to understand a clinical report on hormonal levels. There are two specific subjects that are not usually found in Argentine school curriculums. One of them is vocational training, where students learn how to use computers, how to write a resume and what to do at a job interview. The other one is called education and gender, where topics such as health and biology are addressed with a gender perspective and where they talk about how to prevent HIV/AIDS, among other things. The male professor in charge of that course invited us to participate in a lesson, where he challenged students' perception on physical gendered features that are believed to be natural for men and women, beliefs that perpetuate the naturalization of the gender difference. In that class, he questioned whether it was right or not to think that men were stronger than women, or whether there were cultural or social elements that made women exercise less than men and be, in consequence, less strong. Later, he discussed how gender expectations and roles created ideals of beauty that establish what is normal and what is not.

Right after class, we interviewed one of his students, who was not as critical as him towards gender stereotypes. Discussing a large variety of topics, Participant D said that she worked out so as to be in shape for her job and that she would tone up certain parts of her body (abs, gluteus and legs) to have a more feminine look, and disregard the ones that would her look masculine (arms, back and chest). She told us that she was working in the sex industry at the time but that she was attending school in order to get a more decent job. Speaking about the previous class, she acknowledged that other schools wouldn't discuss subjects like these. She observes that now there is more awareness on transgender issues and that there is less discrimination than before. But in the past, she says, teachers and adults in general had no training or knowledge on gender studies, and there was definitely no social awareness on transgender issues. She thinks that is the reason why they would treat transgender and gender non-conforming students in a discriminatory way, as if they were extraterrestrials or freaks.

Luckily for her and her schoolmates, the Mocha Celis secondary school builds and promotes respectful and equal educational relationships. Its members follow and embrace the pedagogical, institutional and political principles that guide their practice, and they all agree that the school, just like their students, differ from the hegemonic notions of "normal" bodies, desires and sexualities. In other words, the Mocha Celis project is a great example of how certain educational institutions can battle those pedagogical projects that condemn diverse groups to failure and exclusion due to their gender, sexuality, socioeconomic status or ethnicity. Their best lesson is that other universes of political and educational actions and practices are possible and that it is worth fighting for them.

The Mocha Celis trans-baccalaureate is the first Argentine state school that guarantees the recognition of the human rights—and, therefore, the economic, social and cultural rights—of transgender people, homosexuals and more groups that were historically excluded and deliberately doomed to failure in the complex modern education system. Not only does it distance itself from the "norm," but it denounces the oppositional, hierarchical, classificatory and excluding binarism of the modern Argentine educational institutions through its political and educational proposal. With nuances, and not without internal tensions, the Mocha Celis School assumes a clear political position battling for the empowerment and the materialization of real and equal social, cultural, political, legal and economic opportunities for trans people, and for all. It questions the idea of the body as something merely organic, fixed, universal and ahistorical. It sees the body as a locus of dispute in which different social actors and discourses try to impose certain meanings, often coercive, on its sexed materiality. Likewise, it alters the nature of the notion of sexuality as something fixed and already given. It questions the biological determinism that supposes relations and mechanical and linear processes according to the sexed body that one "has." It rejects the subordination of sub-alternized sexual groups as something natural. It identifies the traits of the patriarchal oppression that minorize and stigmatize trans groups. And it objects to certain imaginaries that link transgender people with ideas of deviation, perversion, illness, abuse, immorality and abnormality by questioning the dominant phallogocentric sexual morality.

In short, the school's commitment is complex. It assumes the disobedience and resistance over the traditional political economy of desire and pleasure as a true educational act. Its offer is an invitation to resemanticize bodies, sexualities, desires, pleasures and emotions while sustaining the impossibility of placing them outside of discourses, language, institutions, ideology and culture. It also rejects the sexual dimorphism as a "scientific" truth and the heterosexuality as the only valid and "normal" alternative of desire. It challenges the approach based on the notions of tolerance and respect towards non-hetero-normative groups since this vision leaves intact the categories by which homosexuality, transvestism or transsexualism have historically and socially been defined as abnormal forms of sexuality. That is to say, this matrix of thought would only produce another type of binarism by admitting the existence of the categories of tolerant heterosexuals and of tolerated transsexual, homosexual and *travesti* people. That is what the Mocha Celis School is battling along with its activism and its educational-political bet to promote social change through the protection of trans people's right to education.

ACKNOWLEDGMENTS

We are deeply grateful to all and every single member of the Mocha Celis School. We especially want to thank Principal Francisco Quiñones for opening us the doors of the school and for the information provided. We also want to thank Professor Agustín Fuchs and the 2nd year students (class of 2016) for sharing with us their time and their invaluable testimonies; without them, this research wouldn't have been possible. Additionally, we would like to thank Universidad Nacional de Quilmes and the National Scientific and Technical Research Council (CONICET) for their financial support.

NOTES

1. Law on Sexual Health and Responsible Procreation No. 25673 (2002); National Program of Comprehensive Sex Education, Law No. 26150 (2006); National Education Bill No. 26206 (2006); Curricular Guidelines for Comprehensive Sex Education (2008); Equal Marriage Bill No. 26618 (2010) and the modification of the Civil Code; and Gender Identity Law No. 26743 (2012), to name a few.

2. Adrienne Rich, "La Heterosexualidad Obligatoria y La Existencia Lesbiana," in *Sexualidad, Género Y Roles Sexuales*, comp. Marysa Navarro and Catharine R. Stimpson (Buenos Aires: Fondo De Cultura Económica, 1999).

3. Monique Wittig, *El Pensamiento Heterosexual y Otros Ensayos* (Madrid: Egales, 2006).

4. Paul B. Preciado, *Manifiesto Contrasexual* (Barcelona: Anagrama, 2011).

5. The letters LGBT have been used to refer to all individuals and communities that identify as lesbian, gay, bisexual or transgender or those who are questioning their sexual orientation and/or their gender identity. There is no single way to arrange the letters (GLBT, for example). Some people use additional letters, like I for intersex (formerly known as hermaphrodism), Q for queer or questioning, and A for asexual or to name the allies that are not LGBT but that support them (LGBTQIA).

6. Here we use "trans" or "transgender" in a broad way so as to name all people who are not cisgender. In our text, the students we interviewed identified as transgender, as transvestites, or as both. In Argentina, being a transvestite (*travesti*) is a gender identity that ought not to be mistaken with being a drag queen. For more on this category, see Pedro Di Pietro, "Andar De Costa-

do: Racialización, Sexualidad, y La Descolonización Del Mundo Travesti En Buenos Aires," in *Andar Erótico Decolonial*, comp. Raúl Moarquech Ferrera Balanquet (Buenos Aires: Ediciones Del Signo, 2015).

7. AA. VV. *La Revolución De Las Mariposas. A Diez Años De La Gesta Del Nombre Propio*. (Buenos Aires: Ministerio Público De La Defensa De La Ciudad Autónoma De Buenos Aires, 2017).

8. "For the exercise of these rights the law does not require medical diagnoses to be accredited; it dismantles and condemns any act that disturbs, hinders, denies or injures the rights it contains, and considers it a discriminatory practice. The law considers that the will of the person is sufficient and does not judicialize or administer the right to recognition of their gender identity. The manifestation of the will is done through the use of a simple form where the request for the rectification of the name is recorded and, in the case of surgical interventions, informed consent must be taken. The gender identity law avoids any normative definition of identity categories such as '*travesti*,' 'transsexual' or 'transgender,' to revalue the right to corporal autonomy. It also guarantees the recognition of the gender identity of transgender boys, girls and adolescents in the areas where they carry out their activities, especially how they should be called and registered, the respect for their self-perceived name and access to comprehensive health. For that, it incorporates the figure of the 'child's lawyer' according to current legislation on children and adolescents, which reinforces the protection of the right to corporal autonomy of the child-adolescent subject. With this law, which also includes migrant persons, the Argentine State recognizes the politicity of trans subjectivities: they are no longer instituted as pathological, diseased or dysphoric identities" (our translation, original text: "Para el ejercicio de esos derechos la ley no requiere que se acrediten diagnósticos médicos; desarticula y condena cualquier acto que perturbe, obstaculice, niegue o lesione los derechos que contiene, y lo considera una práctica discriminatoria. La ley considera que la voluntad de la persona es suficiente y no se judicializa ni administrativiza el derecho al reconocimiento de su identidad de género. La manifestación de la voluntad se realiza mediante el uso de un formulario sencillo donde consta la petición para la rectificación del nombre y, para el caso de las intervenciones quirúrgicas, se debe tomar el consentimiento informado. La ley de identidad de género evita cualquier definición normativa de categorías identitarias tales como 'travesti,' 'transexual' o 'transgénero,' para revalorizar el derecho a la autonomía corporal. Garantiza, asimismo, el reconocimiento a la identidad de género de niños, niñas y adolescentes trans en los ámbitos donde desempeñen sus actividades, en especial cómo se los/as debe llamar y registrar, el respeto a su nombre autopercibido y el acceso a la salud integral. Para eso incorpora la figura del 'abogado del niño' de acuerdo a la legislación vigente en materia de infancia y adolescencia, que

refuerza la protección al derecho a la autonomía corporal de la subjetividad infanto-adolescente. Con esta ley, que también incluye a las personas migrantes, el Estado argentino reconoce politicidad a las subjetividades trans: dejan de ser instituidas como identidades patológicas, enfermas o disfóricas"). AA. VV. *Situación De Los Derechos Humanos De Las Travestis y Trans En La Argentina*. Report. October 2016, accessed November 2017, https://tbinternet.ohchr.org/Treaties/CEDAW/Shared Documents/ARG/INT_CEDAW_NGO_ARG_25486_S.pdf.

9. Article 2 of the Law No. 26618/2010 on Civil Marriage (commonly known as the Equal Marriage Bill) establishes that "marriage shall have the same requirements and effects, regardless of whether the parties are of the same or different sex" (our translation; original text: "el matrimonio tendrá los mismos requisitos y efectos, con independencia de que los contrayentes sean del mismo o de diferente sexo").

10. Judith Butler, *Cuerpos Que Importan: Sobre Los Límites Materiales y Discursivos del "Sexo"* (Barcelona: Paidós, 2002), 18.

11. Judith Butler, *El Género En Disputa: El Feminismo y La Subversión de La Identidad* (Mexico: Paidós, 2011).

12. Judith Butler, *Deshacer El Género* (Buenos Aires: Paidós, 2006).

13. Irene Vasilachis De Gialdino, *Estrategias de Investigación Cualitativa* (Buenos Aires: Gedisa, 2007).

14. Pierre Bourdieu, *The Logic of Practice*, trans. Richard Nice (Stanford: Stanford University Press, 2014).

15. We pick up the definitions of "tactics" and "strategies" found in Michel de Certeau, *La Invención De Lo Cotidiano 1: Artes de Hacer*, trans. Alejandro Pescador (Mexico: Universidad Iberoamericana, 2007).

16. Lohana Berkins, "Por Qué La Escuela Se Llama Mocha Celis," *Página 12*, November 18, 2011, accessed November 2017, http://www.pagina12.com.ar/diario/suplementos/soy/subnotas/2201-206-2011-11-18.html.

17. Our translation. Original text reads as follows: "El clima que estamos construyendo es el de la igualdad y para eso no necesitamos la piedad, sino la justicia del Estado." "Bachillerato Trans Mocha Celis," *Otra Buenos Aires*, April 16, 2013, accessed November 2017, http://www.otrabuenosaires.com.ar/bachillerato-mocha-celis-un-paso-hacia-la-igualdad/.

18. Our translation of the text: "Es un modo de educación sumamente inclusivo y alcanza segmentos que quedan fuera de la educación formal. La idea de que sea inclusivo en razón de la identidad sexual es muy importante porque, en todas las investigaciones que llevamos adelante, una de las primeras conse-

cuencias del travestismo es el abandono de la escuela." Julieta Lorea, "El Saber Travestido," El Gran Otro, accessed August 24, 2018, http://elgranotro.com/index.php/el-saber-travestido/.

19. Sabrina Testa, *La Existencia de la Mocha Celis, O, La Visibilidad en la Invisibilidad Educativa* (Buenos Aires: Ediciones La Mariposa Y La Iguana, 2015), 32.

20. Sabrina Testa, *La Existencia de la Mocha Celis, O, La Visibilidad en la Invisibilidad Educativa* (Buenos Aires: Ediciones La Mariposa y La Iguana, 2015).

21. Marina Ampudia, "Movimientos Sociales y Educación: Los Bachilleratos Populares en la Argentina," Contrahegemonía Web, December 13, 2014, accessed November 2017, http://contrahegemoniaweb.com.ar/movimientos-sociales-y-educacion-los-bachilleratos-populares-en-la-argentina/.

22. Ministerio de Educación y Deportes de la Nación Argentina, Dirección Nacional de Información y Estadística Educativa, *Biblioteca Nacional del Maestro,* Florencia Finnegan and María Paula Montesinos, October 2016, accessed November 2017, http://www.bnm.me.gov.ar/giga1/documentos/EL005561.pdf. . 20.

23. AA. VV., "10 Años de Bachilleratos Populares en Argentina," in *Cuadernillo De Debate N°1* (Buenos Aires: GEMSEP, 2015), accessed November 2017, https://drive.google.com/file/d/0B9WAEryqfqZ5MUd4OHRQM2NPMFk/view.

24. Tomaz Tadeu da Silva, *Espacios de Identidad: Nuevas Visiones Sobre El Curriculum* (Barcelona: OCTAEDRO, 2001).

25. Soledad Areal and María Fernanda Terzibachian, "La Experiencia de los Bachilleratos Populares en la Argentina: Exigiendo Educación, Redefiniendo Lo Público," *Revista Mexicana De Investigación Educativa* 17, no. 53 (June 2012), accessed November 2017, http://www.scielo.org.mx/scielo.php?script=sci_arttext&pid=S1405-66662012000200009&lng=es&nrm=iso&tlng=es.

26. Juan Wahren, "Bachilleratos Populares. Las Escuelas Del Pueblo," *Revista Bordes*, November 22, 2016, accessed November 2017, http://revistabordes.com.ar/las-escuelas-del-pueblo/.

27. Lohana Berkins and Josefina Fernández, *La Gesta del Nombre Propio: Informe Sobre la Situación de la Comunidad Travesti en la Argentina* (Buenos Aires: Ediciones Madres De Plaza De Mayo, 2005).

28. Lohana Berkins, comp., Cumbia, Copeteo y Lágrimas: Informe Nacional Sobre La Situación de las Travestis, Transexuales y Transgéneros (Ciudad Autónoma de Buenos Aires: Ediciones Madres de Plaza de Mayo, 2007).

29. According to the definitions that were expressed in the launch of the project, in November 2011, the goals of the Mocha Celis School were: 1. To grant secondary school degrees. 2. To reverse the situation that leads transvestites, transsexuals and transgender people to prostitution. 3. To facilitate the creation of an alternative to prostitution for financial support. 4. To increase the frequency of health controls. To raise awareness about health care. 5. To promote democratic participation and the exercise of full citizenship. 6. To bring transvestites, transsexuals and transgender people to school. 7. To offer specific training that provides knowledge to manage small-sized enterprises and cooperatives that function as a source of income. 8. To increase the quality of life of the transvestite, transsexual and transgender collective of the Autonomous City of Buenos Aires and its surroundings. "Bachillerato Popular Trans Mocha Celis: Desafío Educativo En Marcha," Revista Furias, March 14, 2012, accessed November 2017, http://revistafurias.com/bachillerato-popular-trans-mocha-celis-desafio-educativo-en-marcha.

30. Agustín Fuchs, *El Bachillerato Popular Para Jóvenes y Adultxs Mocha Celis. Experiencias en el Diseño Y Planeamiento de un Bachillerato Popular Para Personas Travestis, Transexuales y Transgéneros*, proceedings of IV Coloquio Internacional Interdisciplinario: Educación, Sexualidades y Relaciones de Género, Facultad de Filosofía y Letras, Buenos Aires (Universidad De Buenos Aires, 2011).

31. Our translation of the text: "Se ha dicho que es una escuela para '*chicas travestis*,' pero decimos que es mucho más; primero porque identidades trans no somos solamente '*chicas travestis*,' hay varones trans, mujeres transgénero, transexuales, hay maneras muy diversa de nominarse y autopercibirse," Belén Spinetta, "Mocha Celis: Un Bachillerato Trans de Puertas Abiertas," *Comunicar Igualdad*, March 18, 2015, accessed November 2017, http://comunicarigualdad.com.ar/mocha-celis-un-bachillerato-trans-de-puertas-abiertas/.

32. Silvia Delfino, "Investigación y activismo en el vínculo entre teorías de género, identidad de géneros y luchas políticas," in *Revista Tram[p]as, 66*, (2009: 36–54).

33. Our translation of the text "en la escuela pública no existe ningún debate, por ejemplo, en el tema del uso de los baños, la gimnasia separada, etc. Todo se enseña desde una óptica hetero-normativa y binaria," Gustavo Pecoraro and Verónica Dema, "Nace El Primer Bachillerato Para Travestis," *Boquitas Pintadas* (blog), February 29, 2012, accessed November 2017, http://blogs.lanacion.com.ar/boquitas-pintadas/agenda/nace-el-primer-bachillerato-para-travestis/.

34. Our translation, original text is as follows: "Una dejaba la secundaria porque te llamaban por tu nombre de varón o tu aspecto era otro, o habías decidido que tu vida sea diferente a la de los demás. Entonces para mí sí, es

eso. Ahora estamos mucho más incluidas en la sociedad y antes no. Para qué ibas a estudiar si en la calle no te piden tener título de nada. ¡Un taco alto y pintura, y ya está!" AA. VV., *La Revolución de las Mariposas. A Diez Años de la Gesta del Nombre Propio* (Buenos Aires: Ministerio Público de la Defensa de la Ciudad Autónoma de Buenos Aires, 2017), 89.

7

TO BE NEW, BLACK, FEMALE, AND ACADEMIC

Renaissance of Womanism within Academia

Vanessa Drew-Branch, Sonyia Richardson, and Laneshia Conner

INTRODUCTION

In Alice Walker's 1983 collection of essays *In Search of Our Mothers' Gardens: Womanist Prose,* Walker introduces the world to Womanism, a sister social theory to Feminism. Womanism considers how intersectionality influences the lives of women of color and provides a framework that legitimizes the narratives of Black women as both women and racial minorities.[1] Womanism does this in a way that Feminism does not because Feminism fails to account for the multi-identity tension that exists for women of color. Womanism, like Feminism, views the experiences of women within patriarchal constructed systems as a central theme. Concurrently, Womanism embraces how the multiple and complex identities of Black women profoundly affect how we interact with our world and how the world responds to us.

What does it mean to be new, Black, and female in a male-dominated industry, such as academia? It means that along with the accumulation of experiences of discrimination and stereotyping this group of academics carry, they are now charged to address institutional racism within higher education not just from a personal but also professional perspective. Black female scholars have entered the academy with hopes that they would be able to build upon and expand not only their own scholarship and pedagogies, yet also the work from historical figures in both the feminist and race equality scholarship. This connection of identity and experience adds a nuanced voice that speaks to the specific intersectional experience of Black women and girls. What does it mean to be fully Black and fully female in a White, male-dominated space? This question has largely gone unanswered because the Black female experience has not been valued as a stand-alone American experience, and therefore, not captured as often as our White counterparts. There are gaps in contemporary academic writings that address the duality with identifying as "one of the most privileged minorities on the planet"—being an academic—and belonging to a sexual/ethnic minority—being female and Black. As higher education adapts to the demand for a more inclusive environment, members of the academic community, faculty, staff, administration and any stakeholders that are affiliated with academic institutions must engage in candid conversations that highlight the presence of Black female scholars and look at the myriad of ways to conceptualize this group in academe. The lives of Black female scholars have been affected by sexual, racial, and class oppression, and, in this chapter, those oppressions will be fleshed out using themes of Womanism to develop an understanding of the impact these oppressions have made, and how up-and-coming scholars can use them to navigate their experiences in higher education.

WOMANISM RENAISSANCE

According to Walker, Womanism was as similar to Feminism as purple is to lavender. Walker first used the term "womanist" in her 1983 work *In Search of Our Mothers' Gardens: Womanist Prose*, where she lays out the foundational understanding of Womanism. In this collection of essays, articles, reviews, statements, and speeches, Walker defines the conceptual framework of Womanist/ism. The term Womanist comes from the term *womanish,* which is opposed to girlish that carries connotations of behaviors that are frivolous, irresponsible, and not serious.[2] Walker wanted to create a term that commanded attention to the seriousness of the plight of women. Walker pulled this term from her experience with the Black vernacular. Womanish is used to describe female children who are behaving like adults. The expression *womanish* is also used to describe behaviors that are considered outrageous, audacious, and courageous or have been socially defined as immoral or illegal. The Womanist theory emphasizes how Black women have been historically contextualized as instruments of production. This theoretical lens situates Black women as (1) a population of African descent in a nation historically and fundamentally rooted in a racialized slave economy; (2) women in a profoundly patriarchal structure; and (3) laborers: productive; reproductive.

Controlling images are a tactic of an oppressive system. Oppressive systems are enduring because they are malleable and pervasive. These images were created to securely root Black women in a laboring class. The laboring class is marked by the domination of the productive, reproductive, and biological agency of Black.[3] The Womanist theory provides a theoretical lens in which race is acknowledged as a concern for Black women and consequently provides a platform for the analysis of race and gender to occur jointly. The Womanist framework acknowledges the historical struggle for the oppression of Black women to be visible on a level comparable to that of the oppressive experiences of Black men and for the unique experiences of Black women not to be silenced by the agenda of White women.

There is a lack of understanding of the theoretical positioning and tenants of the Womanism framework. One of the primary tenants suggests a Womanist is a person who loves women, sexually and nonsexually. Walker explicitly stated that Womanists appreciate and prefer women's culture, women's emotional flexibility, and women's strength.[4] Womanism seeks to state that women, specifically women of color, have a culture that while not separate from a feminist culture has unique experiences that deserve acknowledgment and value. Historically, social movements have overshadowed and ignored the concerns and interests of Black women. The discrimination based on gender that women in America challenged during the woman suffrage movements is nationally celebrated as the "first wave" of the feminist movement of equity and equality. However, there are documented accounts of active and purposeful exclusion of Black women voices from the leaders of the suffragist movement.

The minimization of Black women was also prevalent during the Civil Rights and Black Power movements. For example, in 1964, civil rights activist Stokely Carmichael was quoted as saying that "the only position for women in SNCC (Student Nonviolent Coordinating Committee) is prone."[5] Although Carmichael was speaking at a time when the contributions of women were largely dismissed as unimportant or ineffective, there were many Black women active within the most influential civil rights organizations. Nonetheless, the presence of some did not make them exempt from scrutiny. Some of the most notable leaders within these organizations subscribed to this patriarchal ideology. Roy Wilkins, leader of the National Association for the Advancement of Colored People (NAACP), told women such as Fannie Lou Hamer and other politically active females that they were "ignorant of the political process, should listen to their [male] leaders and return home."[6] Another example can be found with Lawrence Guyot, a prominent SNCC activist who made the suggestion that [Black] women step back and let the men come forth. There are other examples and statements that dismiss the presence and roles of Black women during those critical times, highlighting the discord within race to elevate the stance of Black women and their voices.

Black female scholars such as bell hooks and Patricia Hill Collins have questioned the exclusion of issues unique to Black women within these social movements as well. Black women experienced silencing in both the Black Power and Feminist movements, although they were critical participants in both. Black women were forced to choose race over gender or vice versa, with either choice resulting in their membership and loyalty being challenged. This clash of identities led to many Black women feeling shunned and needing to adjust their way of being.[7] These types of experiences still hold true today, particularly among young, Black female academics. The common biases that work against Black professional women, in general, can be harrowing. The challenges to Black women, such as being torn between authenticity and assimilation, are both internal and external challenges that can become apparent in professional practices and especially important to academics who deal with issues like imposter syndrome and invisibility. To fully understand their current experiences and build professional resilience, using the conceptual framework of Womanism provides a platform for Black women to first define Black woman culture, identity, and freely express self-love.

By applying the lens of Womanism and re-envisioning the historical controlling images that have been used to define experiences of Black women, young, Black female academics will be able to reclaim their identities within the Eurocentric, patriarchal higher education system and be provided tools to shape discussions for restoration of overall appreciation for humanity and good work done. The call for a renaissance of the Womanist perspective as it relates to Black women in higher education is necessary to shift the predominant narrative away from the adverse historical construction of the Black female identity. The Renaissance view includes more complex and nuisance identities that reimagine the negative tropes into positive, strength-based attributes that have contributed and will contribute to the success of Black women in the academic environment. The renaissance of a contemporary Womanist perspective will necessitate viewing the Black female identity through a lens of valuing the unique culture of Black women. As a coping mechanism and positive attribute, resiliency has led to the identification of adaptive behaviors that buffer the effect of these types of stressors. While resiliency may have been a characteristic long standing within the Black community, it brings both positive and negative influences that stem from the social construction of the Black female identity. The social images that depict Black women are influenced by racism and sexism. The construction of the Black female identity has served as a means to keep Black women in a socially subordinate role.

BLACK WOMEN, CONTROLLING IMAGES, AND CREATION OF THE LABORING CLASS

Prototypes have commonly been used to offer observers a snapshot of a person or idea. Albeit too familiar for Black people in academia, standard snapshots are "You are very bright," "You are different," and things that deem them the exception to others in their community. For Black women, this type of labeling carries an additional burden. The construction of Black female archetypes and their social positioning is heavily rooted in the American doctrines of manifest destiny and capitalism.[8] The typification of the "Black female" identity can be dated to African colonization and the slave trade. As a result of justifying and maintaining the horrific system of slavery, this identity was the direct result of the dominant and subjugated relationship, a central relationship that served a critical function to the shaping of Black females in this country. As Patricia Hill Collins has asserted in her work, *Black Feminist Thought*, the history of the U.S. development of the capitalistic system is deeply interconnected to the objectification and exploitation of Black female identity by slave owners.[9] The domination of the Black female identity narrative has led to controlling images of Black women to perpetuate images such as Mammies, Matriarchs, Jezebels, Sapphire, Welfare Queen, and Crack Whore.[10] For Black women, these controlling images have been fixed in subjugation and objectification, further shaping the national and global understanding of Black femaleness. The issues of images are essential, as it dictates our ability to answer questions such as "Who am I, who are we, and who are they?" Being able to control images and their influence has had a profound effect on how our personal and collective identities are formed.

The Jezebel image references the Christian biblical figure about a conniving harlot who worships false gods (Revelation 2:20, King James Version). The Jezebel image justified slavery by portraying African women as subhuman. This image promotes the belief that Black women have insatiable sexual desires and are prone to promiscuity. The inaccurate image portrayed Black women as sexually immoral by nature. Accordingly, they cannot be raped because they enjoy sex under any circumstances. This narrative justified the sexual exploitation of enslaved women.[11] It is removing Black women's ability to control their sexuality allowed slave owners to perpetrate sexual violence against Black women that would result in the birth of children that would increase economic gains for the slave owners. Fast forward to the twenty-first century; we have contemporary versions of the Jezebel image, that include hoochie, video vixens, hoodrats, gold-diggers, and freaks. These terms have been used interchangeably to describe and depict Black sexuality, desirability, and a Black female prototype.

Another controlling image for Black women that is closely related to the Jezebel image is the Crack Whore. The devastating impact of the 1980s and 1990s "War on Drugs" called for the emergence of a specific controlling image for Black women that would explain the disproportionate numbers of Black women who were being affected by the introduction of crack in impoverished Black communities. The image of the Crack Whore is one who is also sexually immoral and so consumed with drug use that she will forgo all the crucial things in life to score drugs. The Crack Whore is an unfit, abusive, and neglectful mother; she is unwilling to clean up her life so that she can maintain personal responsibility. Her lack of will and self-determination is an indicator of her lack of moral character.

The image of the Welfare Queen emerged during the same 1980s and 1990s time period. The political emphasis of the time was cut or end social welfare programs. Just as with the other previously mentioned images, the Welfare Queen image was constructed to meet the economic goals of the dominant group. The image of the Welfare Queen was constructed as a materialistic, domineering, single mother who depended on the government to support her family.[12] The Welfare Queen relied on public funds to support her lifestyle while she continues to have illegitimate children from multiple fathers. The Welfare Queen lies and schemes to retain her government funding so that she can avoid the responsibility of working. The creation of this image was in direct relationship with the political desire to cut spending on federal social service programs but not address the discriminatory education and employment practices that have locked Black women out of opportunities to advance.

The Mammy controlling image emerged after the ending of slavery and cast Black women in the domestic help and caretaking role for White families.[13] An excellent example of this image is depicted in the 2009 book and 2011 movie *The Help* by Kathryn Stockett. This piece of literature and the cinematic rendition depicted the relationship between Black female domestics and their White employers. A "good" maid would sacrifice her own family's needs to meet the needs of the White family she was serving. The Mammy image embodies self-sacrifice. This controlling image encouraged Black women to remain submissive to their oppression and teach their children to remain submissive. The Mammy image is constructed as an overweight, loyal, happy, lazy, unintelligent, asexual being who is not capable of working without the supervision and approval of White employers.

Another closely related Mammy controlling image is the Sapphire image. Sapphire defined what it is to be a "bad" Black woman and mother. This image emerged when Black female-headed homes were becoming more prevalent within the Black community.[14] The Sapphire image is based on the 1940s sitcom character that appeared on *The Amos 'n Andy Show*. Sapphire, who is also a Matriarch, is the feminine archetype that fails to meet her "womanly duties" within her home.[15] This image is characterized as reliable, masculine workhorses who are capable of doing "men's" work. Sapphires are overbearing, overly aggressive, unfeminine women; they emasculated their lovers and husbands, resulting in parenting alone. The Sapphire implies that Black women are supposed to be physically strong and capable of enduring the violence and discrimination they experience. Because Sapphires spend too much time away from home, these working mothers ostensibly could not adequately supervise their children, and this was a major contributing factor to their children's failure at school. This image of Black women detracted from the strain that poverty places on Black communities. Casting Black women as these angry and hostile creatures gave justification for why they were left alone to parent children and the high levels of unemployment or disproportionate concentration in low-wage jobs. This image once again served a capitalistic goal of maintaining a significant supply of low-wage laborers.

One of the most contemporary images of Black women is the "Strong Black Woman" (SBW) or "Ms. Independent."[16] This archetype is closely related to Sapphire, but the significant difference is the level of educational and economical attainment of SBW. In the 1980s and 1990s, despite many historical challenges, a significant number of Black women have attained high levels of education.[17] The research suggests that the wages of Black women are still lagging behind the wage growth of White women, White men, and Black men.[18] Although the wage gaps continue to persist, Black women have made significant gains in closing the employment gaps in many industries. This imagery has led to the rise in economic status for the current generation of Black women who are more highly educated and employed at higher paying positions than in the past. This image has also given rise to the stereotypes that are portrayed in pop culture in such as music videos by Destiny's Child "Independent Women," "Survivor," and Beyoncé's "Single Ladies." The SBW archetype is viewed as harsh, sassy, and hardworking. Unlike the older archetypes, the SBW is viewed as upper-middle class and hyper-focused on material possessions and her physical appearance.[19] SBW is portrayed as caring genuinely for others (i.e., communal), sometimes to the detriment of her personal needs. The SBW archetype is a gendered expression of the "exceptional Negro" or "Talented Tenth."[20] The SBW personifies that the United States is a post-racial society where racism and sexism have diminished to the level of not being relevant. The SBW serves as evidence that affirmative action policies and other racial and gender civil rights protections are no longer relevant, necessary, and are even unconditional. Once again, this archetype aims to serve to silence the textured experiences of Black women and to serve as a catalyst to maintain Black women's subordinate role in the capitalistic society. While Black women have historically been instrumental to advancements in education, the influence of these controlling images has shaped how Black women's presence in education has been perceived, with a profound lack of acknowledging the depths of this influence.

HISTORICAL REPRESENTATION OF BLACK WOMEN IN EDUCATION

Historically, access to education was a means to freedom and liberty for Black women. Education was regarded as a pathway to freedom, and those who demonstrated a degree of literacy were assets for the Black community. Black women played an integral role in active resistance to anti-literacy efforts within the Black community and indeed demonstrated persistence and commitment to increasing knowledge through communal educational efforts. Their efforts resulted in consideration for the needs of the community above their self-interests, invisibility, and perceptions of aggressiveness.

Heather Williams recounts stories of Black women during slavery who defied laws prohibiting the education of Blacks and found ways to ensure that Black children, men, and women could increase literacy through innovative means.[21] Disseminating knowledge was accomplished through a communal approach where slaves carried responsibility for informally teaching each other how to read and write. Women with access to the slaveholder's home would transfer information learned to other slaves and share reading materials. Slaveholders who needed their slaves to perform tasks that required literacy would provide informal educational opportunities primarily designed for White benefit.[22] During this period, Black women were focused on the needs of education within the community and utilized knowledge to transfer information to other Blacks. It was not acceptable for a Black woman to gain education and utilize it for her self-interest. The onus was on the literate Black woman to transfer the knowledge. Through education, Black women began reshaping the images beset upon them, from caretakers to being able to take care of business matters through their ability to read and write.

An example of Black women who are known for creating spaces for advocacy and rights of Black women is Maria W. Stewart. Stewart was born to free Black parents in 1803 in Connecticut and became the first Black woman to speak publicly to White and Black audiences on Black women's rights, provide anti-slavery lectures, and leave copies of her lectures. She boldly professed the need for rights for Black women and access to social institutions, including grocery stores and churches. She utilized her platform to educate all people and to provide a voice for the community. She stated in 1831, "How long shall the fair daughters of Africa be compelled to bury their minds and talents beneath a load of iron pots and kettles?"[23]

Post-slavery, education became a means for ensuring emancipation for Black people.[24] Black women experienced increased access to education; they continued to face extreme resistance. Even Black women who have been more recently been recognized as pioneers as being the architects' public education were rejected and undermined within the education system. For example, in 1862, Mary Jane Patterson became the first Black woman to graduate with a bachelor's degree from Oberlin College. She then went on to become the first Black principal of the Preparatory High School for Negroes in 1871. Within a year of her hiring, she was demoted to assistant principal and replaced by a Black male, Richard Greener. Greener only lasted for one year and then resigned, and Patterson was re-appointed as principal of the school. She maintained this position until 1884 when she resigned. While Patterson was accomplished and broke down barriers, there was resistance in supporting Black female leadership within the educational setting, and her position as principal was removed and replaced by a male because of the beliefs in the inferior leadership capacity and abilities of women.

During the integration of schools, Black women and girls were on the frontlines boldly enrolling and walking into schools where they were not welcome, and their lives were placed in danger. The landmark *Brown vs. Board of Education* of 1954 ruling advocated for the integration of schools by overturning the separate but equal policies and ending racial segregation within schools. Shortly after that, in 1956, Autherine Lucy became the first woman to desegregate the University of Alabama after she was denied enrollment in 1952 because of her race. She experienced threats by White mobs and was taunted by existing students and the university community. In 1954, a six-year-old Black female student named Ruby Bridges helped to desegregate an all-White elementary school and was escorted into the school by her mother and U.S. Marshals due to safety concerns. A similar story is shared by a fifteen-year-old Black female named Dorothy Counts-Scoggins, who in 1957 integrated a high school in Charlotte, North Carolina. She recounts stories of being followed by hundreds of people on her first day, being spit at, and having objects thrown at her. These women faced extreme resistance, and, despite that, they boldly walked through the front doors, sat in the classroom, and were determined to receive an education they desired. Some of these women remained at these schools and overcame the odds, while some women found it too complicated and identified covert strategies for getting their educational needs met.

Black women still face structural inequalities related to equitable compensation, advancement support, opportunities, and equitable invisibility. As an example, Ricks[25] termed the ideal as Black females falling through the cracks and being discounted and ignored regarding their educational needs. While considerable research has occurred focused on the needs of Black males within the educational system, it has failed to advance the educational platform for Black females. Despite the commitment to communal education, threats, and attacks against Black women walking on the frontlines to integrate schools, and advocacy for the race, the educational needs and concerns of Black women and girls have gone largely unrecognized and unheard. As members of the educational community, Black women are expected to maintain this invisibility and submissiveness but also maintain an active role as change agents. Black women are to infantilized in these spaces, to be seen (our bodies used as a number or to check participation boxes) but not to be heard. This tension has created challenges to the way Black female academics approach academic spaces and their work within these environments.

PERCEPTIONS OF BLACK WOMEN IN EDUCATION, SCHOLARSHIP, TEACHING, AND SERVICE

Numerous reports have yielded that being a Black professional woman often means that one is a part of an underrepresented group, an unconscious bias that silences or diminishes the roles of Black women, that their statements are remembered less quickly than their White counterparts, as well as less accurately.[26] Moving into higher education, Black women academics deal with oppression and resistance within academe and are often relegated to faculty positions that are typically untenured, lower ranked, and that offer lower pay, and limited growth.[27] Black women earn approximately 60 percent of all doctorates awarded to Blacks, which suggest that there should also be an increase in the percentage of Black female university and college faculty members.[28] However, as Naomi Schiller has pointed out, Black female scholars face significant challenges once they enter the academy.[29] Despite the relatively small number of Black female faculty members in higher education, they face demands not experienced by their White female counterparts. Black female faculty members find that they are inundated with substantial teaching loads and service requests that take energy away from the ability to produce scholarship. These differential demands, when viewed through an intersectionality lens, can be directly connected with the racial and gender archetypes of Black women. Black female faculty members are finding themselves overwhelmed with students who seek them out as mentors, and this is connected to the Mammy and Strong Black Woman (SBW) archetypes. Black women find themselves being elected to serve on many university committees to serve as the sole person of color and potentially female representative, which can be related to the Sapphire/Matriarch archetype.

Furthermore, the types of scholarship that Black female faculty produce is devalued and placed under heavy and differential scrutiny.[30] This presumption of incompetence can be linked once again to the Mammy archetype. Black women also face differential assessments by their peers and students. With an emphasis on scholarship, people of color have always created theories yet not in a Westernized way—for empiricism that is prescriptive or even elite in nature—yet to make meaning through folk tradition and survival.[31] Using mechanisms such as social observation and historical context are additions that scholarship from people of color have added to the theorizing process yet are still scrutinized in a way that is not as common with White counterparts.[32] This scrutiny influences teaching, as several studies have shown that Black female professors receive lower student evaluation outcomes when presenting the same content to students.[33] The widely held and mostly negatively perceptions of Black women coupled with the increased presence of female and scholars of color have brought about the opportunity to challenging antiqued imagery and assess its impact on Black women within the academy.

WOMANISM AND BLACK WOMEN IN HIGHER EDUCATION

Women, in general, have had a long road to overcoming stereotypes about their education. Stemming back to the late 1800s, it was believed that women who became educated were at increased risk for psychological disruption, that their reproductive systems would be compromised, and that education would masculinize women, to name a few.[34] Following a similar yet different path to segregation, women made social and personal sacrifices to pursue their education. The political and social trends in the early 1900s dictated a subpar experience for women and higher education. The beginning of the twentieth century marked distressing working conditions and social nuances that led to the formation of the American Federation of Teachers.

There is not a focus on the disenfranchisement of Black women in education based on both race and gender. Generally, the oppression of women is not stratified by race, and this led to the misconception that educated White and Black women are synonymous in their experiences in higher education. There is significant variation in the lived experiences of both White and Black women. Adrienne Rich described this variation accurately, that when we look at feminism, it has been seen by the experience of White women, or "White solipsism"—as if Whiteness describes the world. [35] Black feminist thought scholar Patricia Hill Collins offers four themes to describe the uniqueness of Black woman culture. These themes are essential to understand how imagery and perception shape the ways Black women are regarded as higher education community members. The first theme is that empowerment for Black women is achieved by creating self-definitions and self-evaluations to fend off the adverse effects of current, negative representations of Black womanhood. The second is that Black women must confront and deconstruct the intersection of race, class, and gender oppression that currently governs the social and political narrative. The third theme is that Black women should blend their intellectual prowess with activism. The fourth and final theme is Black women acknowledge the strength, energy, and skills that stems from their heritage, as it provides a buffer to the daily discrimination that they endure.

To be in academia, as a Black woman, comes with a perception that she is both an anomaly and a representative of the Black community and culture.[36] It carries a dual task of being educated yet being able to learn and continually be educated in areas. It also means that the stigmas from decades of oppression, discrimination, and White solipsism carry over to current day, and if one is not prepared to address it, empowerment and identity are challenged and repressed. In human service and healthcare fields, female academics of color receive training and mentorship from professionals whose race and background are very different from their own and who have been in the professoriate for a significant amount of time. The challenge of that scenario is that it can lead to a "whitening" of social issues and ideologies that are contradictory to Black culture. Adult learners, in the advent of technology and social media, have been bombarded by cultural depictions and examples of Black female imagery that is sensationalized and influenced by the historical archetypes. Students also bring their own life experiences or lack of with Black women into the classroom. It is through these lens that Black female professors, classmates and other Black female community members are viewed.

Female Black academics are caught in a conundrum of competing with larger public images and perceptions of whom they are while trying to understand whom they have evolved into, as earlier discussed in the archetypes of Black females.

(CLASH OF THE NARRATIVES) VULNERABILITY AND RESILIENCE OF BLACK WOMEN IN EDUCATION

For many years, the research has focused on how the construction of the Black female identity within the laboring class context has contributed to increased vulnerability and risk among young, Black, female academics. The shifting research focus from vulnerability and risk to strength and resilience calls for a reexamination of how the construction of the Black female identity has the capability of serving as a protective factor and promotes resilience within the academic environment. The shift in thinking from why Black female academics may not be doing as well in comparison to their male and White counterparts provides a Western pathological-based assessment of Black females' presence in academia. An alternative view is what are some of the characteristics from these controlling images around Black female identity that can be reclaimed and re-envisioned as factors of resilience and success—the reframing of the Black female identity from negative to positive within the higher education context. By reframing the experiences of oppression and marginality, it is possible to create safer spaces that reduce the effects of oppressive experiences.[37]

Based on the review of the stereotypes that exist for each archetype, what they and other famous media lack is the portrayal of the consistent work ethic, creativity, and myriad of skill sets that Black women have, which are necessary for successful academic careers. For example, re-envisioning the nurturing of the Mammy image as being conducive to providing mentorship that is associated with academic success for people of Color.[38] Likewise, the sexual expression of Jezebel being re-envisioned as having less social stigma related to Black female academic positioning their research within sexually taboo topics.

The conceptual construction of resilience is rooted in how a person, group, or community responds to stress, anxiety, trauma, crisis, or disaster. The widely accepted definition of resilience is the "positive adaptation in the face of adversity."[39] Resilience and adaptive behaviors are best understood when assessed within the social and cultural context. Contemporary research on resilience has questioned the understanding of resilience and has rejected the idea of a single construction of the concept. Emerging literature has denounced understandings of resilience that are skewed toward the hegemonic influence of Western theories of favorable adjustment.[40, 41, 42] Researchers commonly describe resilience as a quality of individuals that reflects their capacity to engage in processes that make it likely they will overcome adversity and achieve normal or exceptional levels of psychosocial development (e.g., they will go to school, maintain a prosocial peer group, and avoid delinquency).[43] Resilience research often overlooks the effect of cultural immersion within the dominant culture and heterogeneity among people of Color. Unger provided an alternative view of resilience in 2011, and it states:

> In the context of exposure to significant adversity, resilience is both the capacity of individuals to navigate their way to the psychological, social, cultural, and physical resources that sustain their well-being, and their capacity individually and collectively to negotiate for these resources to be provided and experienced in culturally meaningful ways. Empirical evidence has examined levels of minority stress in different sub-populations, particularly among black sexual minorities due to the layers of the stigma that they encounter.[44]

The integration of a resilience framework that includes community and cultural factors that contextualize how resilience is defined by Black female academics and how they bring these culturally sensitive factors into the academic space with them is a departure from the previous resilience studies. Utilizing this resiliency framework to view the construction of the Black female identity can serve as an alternative narrative to the presence of Black females in higher education space. Under this premise of resiliency, the Black female controlling images are viewed through the lens of the influence of the capacity of Black female academics to navigate the higher education environment in culturally meaningful ways that sustain their well-being. This shift from risk-focused to resilience-focused narratives will begin to allow Black female academics to seize ownership of their identity narratives. The resilience-focused narrative acknowledges that historically, the Black female identity was constructed and shifted to position Black women in a subordinate status within the labor class. This history must not be overlooked. However, there is an opportunity for young Black academics to assert their identity within the academic space through a resilience-womanist framework.

TOLERANCE AS AN EMBEDDED MEASURE

Qualities that a person may possess that help or hinder them from coping with stress create a part of their agency and make them more, or less, resilient.[45] Resiliency inquiry derives from a phenomenological identification, examining the characteristics of survivors who have experienced high-risk situations.[46] Used as a theory to understand better what makes a person resilient, this theory has evolved to include contextual factors that affect one's well-being. Moreover, for one to understand what makes a person or group resilient, one must identify what the characteristics are that make a person resilient, as opposed to those characteristics that identify a person as self-destructive. In addition, it is strengths-based, as it examines how people tolerate and overcome high-risk situations. How are resilient qualities acquired? This question might be answered by considering the adversity that individuals face and how they endure that situation. Lastly, there is an innate resilience that lies within everyone and can be interpreted as a form of self-righting.[47]

Culture can largely dictate resiliency, as the norm and values that are mainly adopted individually affect characteristics. As aforementioned, the notion of professional resilience among Black women has not only been dictated by racial culture, yet also the professions under which they occupy. That duality can challenge the multiple identities that Black women navigate. Conversely, quantifying resilience regarding positive life indicators can be misleading because standard resilient outcomes (e.g., physical, social, psychological qualities of life) do not necessarily encompass qualities that are deemed of cultural importance to Black women. For example, there is the empirical support that Black women in higher education face "multiple jeopardies with the intersection of race, class, and gender exclusion in mainstream education."[48] By achieving academic and professional success, Black women have had to create dual personas that lead to resilience inside and outside of the classroom.[49] Cultural-specific indicators of quality of life that go beyond traditional resiliency factors, such as how one manages minority stress, sexism, and the harsh reality of being a Black woman in the workplace, can contribute to the importance of reframing the narrative.

CONTEMPORARY POSITIONING OF BLACK WOMEN IN HIGHER EDUCATION

Doctorate recipients are examples of the intellectual capacity of not only a university but also of the education system in the U.S. Doctoral work signifies the investment that is required for individuals to develop and contribute to knowledge-generation and creation; this process is a hallmark of this nation. An example of the merit of the doctoral education is demonstrated by the number of international students, who are top students in their countries of origin, that come to the United States to be trained and educated in their fields of study. Over time, there has been an increased representation of people of color and women receiving a doctoral degree.

As a reflection of this country's doctoral system, as well as the political, social, demographic, and economic trends in the country, newly minted academics of color should understand their presence in the educational system, as they are a traditionally underrepresented group. As of 2014, there are increasingly more women receiving doctorates, with this group being awarded 46 percent of earned doctorates.[50] Over the past two decades, Blacks or African Americans have grown from 4.1 percent in 1994 to 6.4 percent in 2014 as doctorate recipients.[51] In non-science and engineering fields, the presence of female doctorate recipients has increased at a much slower rate compared to those in science and engineering fields, with more than half (57 percent) of the non-science and engineering field doctorates being awarded to women. African Americans comprise of the largest ethnic group in education and non-science and engineering fields, and act as the primary points of contact for adult learners in higher education. That says something about who the scientific and theoretical contributors and influencers are in fields such as social work, human services, psychology, and women and gender studies. These statistics communicate something about the uphill battle that scholars of color have overcome to position themselves as intellectuals in academia. While this presence was growing, also a complementary group of intellectuals is growing as well.

In the advent of technology, the look and voice of knowledge-generation and creation have evolved. Technology has propelled a school of contemporary intellectuals of color, and they have contributed to how we conceptualize intelligence, creating a new indicator of intellectual capacity. Having examples such as Toni Morrison, bell hooks, Melissa Harris-Perry, and Cornel West, all of whom are academicians, to literary intellectuals such as Ta-Nehisi Coates and Jamilah Lemieux, have expanded the scope of what defines Black intelligence. By making their names with their online presence, a term coined by Michael Eric Dyson as "Black digital intelligentsia," their ideologies and perspectives go beyond the realms of campuses through social, medical vehicles that are important to them and generations who are not as familiar or connected with the academy. This blending of intellectual power has increased what has been defined as scholarship, activism, and social justice because it brings thinkers together that would otherwise be separate. Looking at the products from the Black Lives Matters movement, wherein intellectuals from both the academy and mainstream media could interact and create links to stimulate attention and awareness regarding the unjust use of authority by law enforcement, the contemporary Black intellectual has become a growing landscape. This group of intellectuals should also be considered when we are discussing intellectuals, as they affect how knowledge is defined and generated as well.

The struggles that have been faced over the decades regarding accessing higher education and the resources necessary to increase graduation rates has raised awareness around needs that remain for academics of color. It was recently revealed that when examining doctoral students in STEM fields, most of the Black and Latino students were not earning their degrees within seven years and were leaving their programs.[52] For those who completed their degrees, the keys to their success included close mentoring relationships with diverse faculty members who provided clear expectations and reviewed their progress regularly.[53] In other words, the mentoring relationship required critical attention and intentional action plans to position students of color to have clear expectations and create balance with the workload demands. Additional experiences occurring in the lives of students of color that are not experienced by their white counterparts can create barriers that truncate their progression and academic growth. These are items for discussion in the mentoring relationship.

In contrast, things that were a hindrance to them was feeling pressure to outperform their peers because they were a member of a racial/ethnic group, the perception that they had to do better than other students, and lack of knowledge from their families about what their pursuit of doctoral education really was.[54] For academics of color, it remains challenging to establish oneself in academia. Despite the increase in African Americans holding master's level and doctoral degrees and participating as faculty and staff in higher education, there is still resistance in accepting their presence on university campuses. Higher education's commitment to access, inclusion and equity present an opportunity for introspective analysis into the current treatment of Black female campus community members. This is a pivotal time for the high educational system to become an influential force, an ally, in the reshaping the social imagery of Black women.

CULTIVATING AND ACKNOWLEDGING PROFESSIONAL RESILIENCE: RE-ENVISIONING THE CONTROLLING IMAGES

So, what does it mean to be new, Black, and female in a White male-dominated industry such as academia? Transformation into this new role requires a re-envisioning of the controlling images that were originally constructed to destroy, confine, and limit Black women. The renaissance of the Womanism theory applied to the academic life of Black female academics will re-envision the images that were meant to oppress and subjugate Black women and create images that serve the collective higher good. It is essential to re-envision each of the negative images through a womanist lens with a resiliency focus.

Table 7.1.

Controlling Image	*Historical Definition*	*Historical Purpose*	*Renaissance Definition*	*Higher Education Womanism Renaissance Purpose*
Jezebel a.k.a. hoochie, video vixen, hoodrat, gold-diggers, and freak	Jezebel is defined as subhuman. Black women have insatiable sexual desires and are prone to promiscuity.	Allowed slave owners to perpetrate sexual violence against Black women that would result in the birth of children. The reproductive lives of slave women were connected to increased economic gains for the slave owners.	Black women are in command of their sexuality. They are accepting of their body image and are comfortable with their sexual expression.	Black women maintain control of their research and scholarship in academia. They are more prone to research taboo or unpopular topics in order to expose oppression and domination. They attempt to resist conformance, which may be viewed as a way of academia attempting to maintain control and power.
Crack Whore a.k.a. Junkie	Crack Whore is defined as lacking good moral judgment and so consumed with drug use that she will forgo all the important things in life to score drugs. The Crack Whore lacks will and self-determination.	Justify the disproportionate numbers of Black women who were faced with the consequences of the "War on Drugs" such as mass incarceration, lack of adequate drug treatment facilities, and ineffective parenting.	Black women are consumed with high standards and resisting mediocrity. They are accountable for high production levels in research, scholarship, and service. They make personal sacrifices with family and life commitments in order to ensure others' needs are met.	Black women are influential leaders in the academic setting and are not afraid to make critical decisions. Thus, they may not be perceived as team players. They exceed expectations for the academic workload and thus may be intimidating to other colleagues and students.
Welfare Queen	The Welfare Queen's image is defined as a materialistic,	This image justified cuts to spending on federal social	Black women are independent and significant contributors to	Black women display a strong work ethic that is demonstrated

Controlling Image	*Historical Definition*	*Historical Purpose*	*Renaissance Definition*	*Higher Education Womanism Renaissance Purpose*
	domineering, single, mother who depends on the government to support her family. This image demonstrates a lack of personal responsibility and good judgment.	service programs but did not address the discriminatory education, employment, and criminal justice practices.	family and society. They maintain responsibility and accountability with their commitments. Black women are assertive advocates for the needs of students, faculty, staff, and the community. Their involvement with advocacy provides them with access to institutional resources; they are viewed as competent and trusted to manage resources.	through hours spent mentoring students, collaborating with colleagues, and participating in activities that are not viewed as self-promoting but benefit their academic units and/or institutions.
Mammy	Mammy is defined as self-sacrificing, submissive, loyal, unintelligent, lazy, happy servants.	This image justified the mistreatment and economic oppression experienced by Black female domestic workers. It supported the notion of Black women being caretakers for everyone, serving the role of a selfless agenda.	Black women maintain healthy boundaries and serve as leaders in the community, church, and employment settings. They consider future generations with decision making. Black women are sought after for committee and service work due to their commitment to	Black women are requested to participate in a more substantial number of service activities than their White male counterparts. However, they are willing to reject requests that do not align with their purpose or interests. When they do contribute, it is

Controlling Image	*Historical Definition*	*Historical Purpose*	*Renaissance Definition*	*Higher Education Womanism Renaissance Purpose*
			the unit, university, and community.	of a high standard. Thus, they are very particular about where they invest their time.
Sapphire a.k.a. Matriach	Sapphire image is characterized as physically strong, masculine workhorses who can do "men's" work. Sapphires are aggressive women who are overbearing and overly aggressive, unfeminine women; they emasculate their lovers and husbands, resulting in parenting alone.	This image of Black women detracted from the strain that poverty places on Black communities. The Sapphire image provides justification for high levels of unemployment or excessive concentration in low-wage jobs.	Black women are nurturing and supportive. They recognize their vulnerabilities and are willing to acknowledge their pain. They forgive yet are protective. They provide an alternative narrative to femininity.	In academia, Black women are excellent mentors and are willing to support others through their pain. They are resilient through this pain and discomfort and express it through a variety of means. They are sought after nurturers, advisors, and advocates. They are viewed as campus champions because of the challenging issues they are willing to confront.
Strong Black Woman (SBW)	The SBW archetype is viewed as harsh, sassy, and hardworking. Unlike the older archetypes, the SBW is viewed as an upper-middle class and hyper-focused on material	This image is used to detract from the persistent struggles within the Black community around poverty-related issues. This image provides a "post-racial" narrative	Black women maintain balance and practice self-care. They recognize that their work, no matter how well done, may not receive the same accolades. They accept that their personal work	In academia, Black women show a strong commitment to the success of their students, colleagues, and academic units. They learn to praise each other collectively and seek support

Controlling Image	*Historical Definition*	*Historical Purpose*	*Renaissance Definition*	*Higher Education Womanism Renaissance Purpose*
	possessions and her physical appearance.	that suggests that structural and social racial inequalities have been eradicated.	and products may not be pleasing to everyone. They accept that they must be their biggest supporters.	from within the community as validation of their work and efforts.

This table represents the shift from the historical definitions and purposes of the controlling images of Black women to the reimagined renaissance definitions and purposes of those same images.

Jezebel

The historical definition of this image defines Black women as subhuman. Black women have insatiable sexual desires and are prone to promiscuity. The historical purpose of this image was that it allowed slave owners to perpetuate sexual violence against Black women, which would result in the birth of children and the reproductive lives of the slave women beings connected to increased economic gains for the slave owners.

The new Renaissance definition of Jezebel envisions Black women being in total command of their sexuality. They are accepting of their body image and are comfortable with their sexual expression. In academia, the Jezebel image has an essential purpose as it encourages Black women in academia to focus their research on taboo topics. They are willing to focus on subjects that are not popular or mainstream and do not seek conformance. They fully embrace their unique Black female contributions and do not shy away from issues that call for an intersectional identity perspective. This image gives them freedom in academic spaces and the courage to challenge the current ideas that are considered "valuable scholarly contributions."

Crack Whore

The historical definition of this image defines Black women as lacking good morals and judgment, is sexually immoral, and so consumed with drug use that she will forgo all the critical things in life to score drugs. The purpose of this image was to justify the disproportionate numbers of Black women who navigate the devastating consequences of the "War on Drugs" such as mass incarceration and lack of adequate drug treatment facilities.

The new renaissance definition of Crack Whore signifies Black women are accountable for high production levels in research, scholarship, and service. They make reasonable personal sacrifices with family and life commitments in order to ensure they maintain a healthy work-life balance, with a strong emphasis on health and the environment. Black women are influential leaders in the academic setting and are not afraid to make critical decisions. However, they are viewed as valuable assets to their units and the university. Their commitment to the success of their work positions them as a valuable contributing team player.

Welfare Queen

The historical definition of this image defines Black women as materialistic, domineering, single mothers who depend on the government to support her family. This image demonstrates a lack of personal responsibility and good judgment. The purpose of this image was utilized to justify cuts to spending on federal social service programs but not to address the discriminatory education and employment practices.

The new renaissance definition views Black women as independent and significant contributors to the educational system. They maintain responsibility and accountability with their commitments. Black women are assertive advocates for the needs of students, faculty, staff, and the community. Their diligence and commitment to their community is viewed as an indicator of competence and trustworthiness. These strengths increase her ability to gain access to and control of university resources.

Mammy

The historical definition of this image identifies Black women as self-sacrificing, submissive, loyal, unintelligent, lazy, happy servants. The purpose of this image was to justify the mistreatment and economic oppression experienced by Black female domestic workers.

The new renaissance definition views Black women as maintaining healthy boundaries and serving as leaders in the community, church, and employment settings. Often, they are sought after for critical decision making. They consider future generations with decision making. Black women are sought after for committee and service work due to their commitment to the unit, university, and community. They have the ability to establish productive relationships with major campus and community stakeholders that are mutually beneficial to all parties.

Sapphire

The historical definition of this image defined Black women as reliable, masculine workhorses who are capable of doing "men's" work. Sapphires are aggressive women who are overbearing and overly aggressive, unfeminine women; they emasculated their lovers and husbands, resulting in parenting alone. The purpose of this image was to detract from the strain that poverty places on Black communities. The Sapphire image justifies high levels of unemployment or disproportionate concentration in low-wage jobs.

The new renaissance definition views Black women as nurturing and supportive. Black women are resilient through pain and discomfort and express it through a variety of means. The re-envisioned Sapphire is a great emphasis on achievement. She often meets or exceeds promotion and tenure goals. Despite the production demands, she maintains strong and rich relationships to her campus community and is engaged with community service–related activities. She is the campus champion for increasing social justice, inclusion and equity for all campus community members.

Strong Black Woman

The historical definition of this image defined Black women as fierce, sassy, and hardworking. Unlike the older archetypes, the SBW is viewed as an upper-middle class and hyper-focused on material possessions and her physical appearance. The purpose of this image is to detract from the persistent struggles within the Black community around poverty-related issues. This image provides a "post-racial" narrative that suggests that structural and social racial inequalities have been resolved because of the level of success that they have achieved.

The new renaissance definition views Black women as maintaining balance and practicing self-care. They accept that their work and products may not be pleasing to everyone. However, the construct their work with the idea of advancing the collective good. Through collaborations, they expand their networks of allies. Black women demonstrate a strong commitment to the success of their students, colleagues, and academic units while seeking out useful mentorship relationships to continue to advance their personal growth.

CONCLUSION

In conclusion, the lack of Black female academics, in a White male-dominated industry such as academia, present challenges that are reinforced by stereotypes and historical references to role-specific norms that can impede their experiences, progress, and persistence. Furthermore, being Black and a female academic poses additional threats to livelihood, productivity, and mental well-being, as the balance of expectations is often under-emphasized or unaddressed in mentoring spaces.

We have highlighted the importance of identifying how Womanist theory plays a significant role in understanding who we are in the academy. Investigating the intersection of race and gender in the academy uncovers bias, and oppressive behaviors and attitudes encountered framed within a historical context. Additionally, acknowledgment of the contributions of Black women in shaping education further provides counterarguments to the negative connotations of Black female academics.

Affirming the roles of Black women in academia through a renaissance of labels and definitions that embolden them ushers in a more positive holistic view of their collective contributions and significant presence in this arena. It positions Black women to embrace these new labels as a means of persistence and motivation through spaces that are not always welcoming and receptive. These redefined labels purposes to dispel old myths and stereotypes that sought to make Black women invisible, unfit, and unmerited.

As we continue to support, promote, and advocate for Black women in higher education, the strengths possessed by this group are recognized, validated, and utilized to assist with movement along the professional continuum. While there remains some debate on the narrative of Black female academics and how their resiliency is a by-product of being immersed in a dominant culture, the resiliency framework provides us with an understanding on how the historical purpose of Black women in education has transformed into the renaissance purpose of this same group of women. The ability to take the controlling images and redefine them as positive, affirming depictions of Black women will be vital in supporting new academics, especially those who do not have adequate mentoring or support in place. These new definitions can catapult this group and other minority academics into equal and safe spaces. The renaissance of Black female imagery and application of Womanist theory will shift the way they are viewed on their campuses. The positive re-envisioning of Black women will deepen the understanding of their unique experiences within the academy. It will signal to the academy that this group requires an equal standing within the higher education. The re-envisioning will equip Black women and their campus communities with the knowledge they have been present and made a valuable contribution to education from the very beginning. Finally, the renaissance of Womanism that asserts a love for Black female culture will demand that Black women have a place at the table and that they are valued.

NOTES

1. Alice Walker, *In Search of Our Mothers' Gardens: Womanist Prose.* (New York: Harcourt, 1983).

2. On this point, see Judith Grant, *Fundamental Feminism: Contesting the Core Concepts of Feminist Theory.* (London: Routledge, 1993): 64.

3. Nicole Rousseau, "Historical Womanist Theory: Re-visioning Black Feminist Thought." *Race, Gender & Class* (2013): 191–204.

4. Ibid., 65.

5. Sabina Peck, "'The Only Position for Women in SNCC Is Prone': Stokely Carmichael and the Perceived Patriarchy of Civil Rights Organisations in America." *History in the Making, 1,* no. 1 (2012): 29–35.

6. Walker, *In Search of Our Mothers' Gardens.*

7. Gabriella Gutiérrez y Muhs, Yolanda Flores Niemann, Carmes G. González, and Angela P. Harris, *Presumed Incompetent: The Intersections of Race and Class for Women in Academia.* (Louisville, UT: Utah State Press, 2012): 88.

8. See Patricia Hill Collins, *Black Feminist Thought: Knowledge, Consciousness, and the Politics of Empowerment.* (Boston: Unwin Hyman, 1990).

9. Ibid., 70.

10. Hill Collins and Carolyn West have focused on controlling images in their works. Carolyn West, "Mammy, Jezebel, Sapphire, and Their Homegirls: Developing an 'Oppositional Gaze' Toward the Images of Black Women." (2012): 286–99.

11. Windsor, Cambraia, Dunlap, and Golub, "Challenging Controlling Images, Oppression, Poverty, and Other Structural Constraints: Survival Strategies among African-American Women in Distressed Households," *Journal of African American Studies, 15,* no. 3 (2011): 290–306.

12. See Hill Collins, *Black Feminist Thought.*

13. Hill Collins, West, and Windsor et al. have produced important work on this trope.

14. Patricia Hill Collins, *Black Sexual Politics: African Americans, Gender, and the New Racism.* (London: Routledge, 2004).

15. Nargis Fontaine, "From Mammy to Madea, an Examination of the Behaviors of Tyler Perry's *Madea* Character in Relation to the Mammy, Jezebel, and Sapphire Stereotypes." (Thesis: Georgia State University, 2011).

16. See Hill Collins, *Black Sexual Politics* and Regina Romero, "The Icon of the Strong Black Wwoman: The Paradox of Strength." In L. C. Jackson and B. Greene (Eds.), *Psychotherapy with African American Women: Innovations in Psychodynamic Perspective and Practice* (New York: Guilford Press): 225–38.

17. Bachman and DiPrete, 2006; C. Freeman, 2004; L. Horn, 1995.

18. Becky Pettit and Stephanie Ewert, "Employment Gains and Wage Declines: The Erosion of Black Women's Relative Wages since 1980," *Demography, 46,* no. 3 (2009): 469–92.

19. Roxanne A. Donovan, "Tough or Tender: (Dis) Similarities in White College Students' Perceptions of Black and White Women," *Psychology of Women Quarterly, 35*, no. 3 (2011): 458–68.

20. William Edward Burghardt Du Bois, "Of Booker T. Washington and Others." *The Souls of Black Folk* (1903): 34–45.

21. Heather Williams, *Self-Taught: African American Education in Slavery and Freedom.* (Chapel Hill: University of North Carolina Press, 2009).

22. Kimberly Sambol-Tosco, "The Slave Experience: Education, Arts, & Culture." *Slavery and the Making of America* (Media with Impact, 2004): https://www.thirteen.org/wnet/slavery/experience/education/history.html, accessed January 15, 2018.

23. Erin Blakemore, "This Little Known Abolitionist Dared to Speak in Public against Slavery, TIME, accessed May 9, 2018, https://time.com/4643126/maria-stewart-abolitionist/.

24. Daphne C. Watkins, B. Lee Green, Patricia Goodson, Jeffrey Joseph Guidry, and Christine A. Stanley. "Using Focus Groups to Explore the Stressful Life Events of Black College Men," *Journal of College Student Development, 48*, no. 1 (2007): 105–18.

25. Shawn Arango Ricks, "Falling through the Cracks: Black Girls and Education," *Interdisciplinary Journal of Teaching and Learning, 4*, no. 1 (2014): 10–21.

26. Ellen McGirt, "Support Black Women at Work," Fortune.com, accessed on May 4, 2019,http://fortune.com/2019/03/05/support-black-women-at-work/black-women-at-work/.

27. Ricks, "Falling through the Cracks."

28. Naomi Schiller, "A Short History of Black Feminist Scholars," 2000.

29. Ibid.

30. American Association of University Women, (2016, April), *The Color of Leadership: Barriers, Bias, and Race.* Retrieved fromhttp://www.aauw.org/2016/04/19/color-of-leadership/.

31. Barbara Christian, "The Race for Theory," *Cultural Critique*, no. 6 (1987): 51–63. doi:10.2307/1354255.

32. Amy Cappiccie, Janice Chadha, Muh Bi Lin, and Frank Snyder, "Using Critical Race Theory to Analyze How Disney Constructs Diversity: A Construct for the Baccalaureate Human Behavior in the Social Environment Curriculum," *Journal of Teaching in Social Work, 32*, no. 1 (2012): 46–61. Amy Cappiccie, Janice Chadha, Muh Bi Lin, and Frank Snyder, "Using Critical Race Theory to Analyze How Disney Constructs Diversity: A Construct for the Baccalaureate Human Behavior in the Social Environment Curriculum," *Journal of Teaching in Social Work, 32*, no. 1 (2012): 46–61.

33. See Lilienfield, 2016, and Perry, Wallace, Moore, and Perry-Burney, 2015.

34. National Women's History Museum [NWHM], 2007.

35. Adrienne Rich, *Disloyal to Civilization: Feminism, Racism, Gynephobia* (NY: W. W. Norton, 1979).

36. Janelle Williams and Ayana Hardaway. "The Metaphysical Dilemma: Academic Black Women," Diverse Issues in Higher Education, accessed on May 3, 2018, https://diverseeducation.com/article/127139/.

37. Mary V. Alfred. "Reconceptualizing Marginality from the Margins: Perspectives of African American Tenured Female Faculty at a White Research University," *Western Journal of Black Studies, 25*, no. 1 (2001): 1.

38. Jessica Henderson Daniel,"Next Generation: A Mentoring Program for Black Female Psychologists," *Professional Psychology: Research and Practice, 40*, no. 3 (2009): 299.

39. Ingrid Schoon and John Bynner, "Risk and Resilience in the Life Course: Implications for Interventions and Social Policies," *Journal of Youth Studies, 6*, no. 1 (2003): 21.

40. Jo Boyden . "Children Under Fire: Challenging Assumptions about Children's Resilience," *Children Youth and Environments, 13*, no. 1 (2003): 1–29.

41. Nora Didkowsky, Michael Ungar, and Linda Liebenberg. "Using Visual Methods to Capture Embedded Processes of Resilience for Youth across Cultures and Contexts," *Journal of the Canadian Academy of Child and Adolescent Psychiatry, 19*, no. 1 (2010): 12.

42. Michael Ungar and Linda Liebenberg, "Assessing Resilience across Cultures Using Mixed Methods: Construction of the Child and Youth Resilience Measure," *Journal of Mixed Methods Research, 5*, no. 2 (2011): 126–49.

43. Alfred, "Reconceptualizing Marginality from the Margins: Perspectives of African American Tenured Female Faculty at a White Research University," 2001.

44. Ungar, 225.

45. Ilan Meyer, "Resilience in the Study of Minority Stress and Health of Sicual and Gender Minorities," *Psychology of Sexual Orientation and Gender Diversity, 2*, no. 3 (2015): 209–13. Retrieved from https://www.apa.org/pubs/journals/features/sgd-sgd0000132.pdf.

46. Glenn E. Richardson, "The Metatheory of Resilience and Resiliency," *Journal of Clinical Psychology, 58*, no. 3 (2002): 307–21.

47. See Richardson "The Metatheory of Resilience and Resiliency," 2002, as well as Emmy E. Werner and Ruth S. Smith, *Overcoming the Odds: High Risk Children from Birth to Adulthood*. Cornell University Press, 1992.

48. Shawn O. Utsey, Mark A. Bolden, Yzette Lanier, and Otis Williams III, "Examining the Role of Culture-Specific Coping as a Predictor of Resilient Outcomes in African Americans from High-Risk Urban Communities," *Journal of Black Psychology, 33*, no. 1 (2007): 75–93.

49. Lisa Bowleg, Jennifer Huang, Kelly Brooks, Amy Black, and Gary Burkholder, "Triple Jeopardy and Beyond: Multiple Minority Stress and Resilience Among Black Lesbians," *Journal of Lesbian Studies, 7*, no. 4 (2003): 87–108. doi:10.1300/j155v07n04_06.

50. National Science Foundation, (2015, December), *Doctorate Recipients from U.S. Universities 2014* (NSF 16-300). Retrieved from https://www.nsf.gov/statistics/2016/nsf16300/digest/nsf16300.pdf.

51. Ibid.

52. Ibid.

53. Scott Jaschik, "Missing Minority PhDs," *Inside Higher Education*, accessed December 6, 2017, https://www.insidehighered.com/news/2014/11/03/study-finds-serious-attrition-issues-black-and-latinodoctoral-students.

54. Ibid.

8

A REJECTION OF WHITE FEMINIST CISGENDER ALLYSHIP

Centering Intersectionality

Beth Hinderliter and Noelle Chaddock

This is a call for those doing conscious social justice work to problematize, if not reject, concepts of allyship in communal spaces of solidarity. Allyship, as currently defined within many feminist spaces, is a detriment to, rather than a bridge towards, an antiracist, multiplicitious, trans welcoming, different ability accommodating, queer-led, anti-imperialist, decolonial feminism. A product of privilege and whiteness in its narrowest sense, allyship gains meaning only within hegemonic structures of oppression, rather than in opposition to these forces. In other words, allyship does not and cannot exist without direct attachment to the oppression, suppression or suffering of the object of the allyship. Thus, allyship needs to also be examined for the ways it might be contributing to the subjugation or objectification of the very individuals and groups it is intended to support and advocate for.

As white and black co-authors engaged in a project of solidarity building, we ask you to consider allyship as coded, privileged, majoritarian, and oppressive—that is, when it is highlighted or asserted, you can probably be sure it isn't happening. As quickly as it is asserted, it can be rescinded, even if we demand that allyship be performed as a verb rather than awarded (often self-awarded) as an identity, as a noun. We might also problematize the timing of said assertions and be mindful of their actual impact on the ally-subject.

We are invoking this *ally-subject* and a few other ally hyphenated words to give a more accessable landscape to the insidiousness of allyship. The ally-subject is necessarily the object, focus and often obsession of said ally in an inequitable, if not dominating and colonial, relationship where the ally's social or ally-capital is dependent on the ally-subject remaining in the oppressive and inequitable situation. We ask you to think with us about the ways that allyship, especially in white cisgender women, is activated and mechanized as violence against transwomen, non-binary women, women with different abilities, international women and women of color. While intersectionality was initially posited to refuse the ways in which feminism did not speak to and incorporate the needs of all women, it is often now neutralized by diversity rhetoric that invokes, but does not enact, intersectional thought and action. Mainstream diversity work focuses on individualism advancing the concerns of the privileged, while marginalizing the values of mutual connectivity, shared responsibility, and interdependent well-being needed to counter this dominance.

In this work, we talk about *white feminism* as it is our assertion that no matter how you frame "feminism," intersectional or not, it is still a performance of white domination and privilege that goes unseen as such by the "women" leveraging their privilege in that space. As we saw with alarming frequency over the summer of 2018, numbers of BBQ Beckys used the police as their personal weapons against people of color.[1] One stark example of this is a professor who called the police on her neighbor because, she says of a noise issue, but in the exchange it became clear that issues of race and class were at play. This professor teaches feminism and intersectionality and is known as an ally on her campus. In her apology, she invokes her allyship as a defense. This and many other examples start to tease out ways in which white cis-gender allyship falls away when women of color, transwomen and international women enter the "women's rights space" where non-white, non-cisgender, non-English speaking people in those spaces are asked to leave all but their womanhood behind. We would like to acknowledge that we are not taking up the issues of black and brown cis-gender women and the violence they too leverage against transwomen in these spaces. This is a necessary and worthwhile conversation that for the sake of time won't be addressed here, but must be picked up with equal attention.

We seek to problematize this conception of allyship in the particular space and performance of women's rights movements in the United States, in particular in the recent "women's marches" that arose out of the Trump election win in 2016. The problems revealed in those marches continue to frame our current political climate, including the threat to the very right for those except a narrow few to identify as women at all in November 2018. The Women's March on Washington crowded the DC mall with pink pussy hat–wearing protesters back in January 21, 2017. Many of them were newly "woke" that previous November, having come of age during the supposed post-racial climate of Barack Obama's eight years in office. Many, however, characterized themselves as battle hardened, seeing in that particular moment recognizable and familiar threats to women's human rights. If that swarm of activism seeking to defend women's rights was a heartening sight for some, it alienated many women of color, whose interests, lives and experiences were marginalized. Here was a group of people united in opposition to domination who had in large part failed to show up for the recent rallies and uprisings that insisted that Black Lives Matter. Many of the larger walks in other urban areas were also fraught with the visual realities that women of color and women in the LGBTQAI community were either missing or underrepresented. In places with majority black populations, the walks still appeared particularly white. As we have started talking about this with women of color in the academy, many have shared with us that they either avoided, if not boycotted, the walk. For many it was not enough that the walks started to add women of color to their front-facing efforts as a second thought. Most damaging, we have found, were the responses from white feminists and march organizers that suggested women of color and transwomen should have just known that they were included because it was for all women. And, of course, all women have the same need for the same rights . . . right? Theses slippages continued in the fall of 2018 when another set of marches were organized, this time just a couple of weeks after an organized March for Black Women. There was a similar lack of white ally support and presence at the March for Black Women, and the following marches were similarly lacking black women as well as other women of color. Yet there is still an insistence that there is a unified effort, an ally relationship extended from white feminists to all non-white feminists and a narrative that feminism represents the interests of all women.

We will not rehash the social media storm around the exclusionary and essentialist "women's marches" but would like to bring responses from white feminists into the conversation. That 2017 response was consistently pointing to this narrowing of the "women's march" space by saying things like "this is for all women," "this is not about race," and "allys are welcome." These responses left many women of color, trans, and non-binary women disenfranchised and not buying the pussy hat. These responses also point to the privilege and dominance of white cis-gender feminists in what are framed as feminist spaces. We are really interested in the slippage between "all women are welcome" and the proud allyship that is then produced from the same space for gay marriage, but not for the Black Lives Matter movement or the inclusion of transwomen in women's reproductive justice agendas. We wonder if women of color and transwomen pushing back against the marches, and the performance of "feminist blindness" that was offered as a response, has damaged an already fragile connection between white cis-gender feminists and those they believe are in need of their "allyship." We also need to unpack the unresolved and long-standing tensions between white women and black and brown women in the United States brought forward in this moment—from slavery and the lived realities of the antebellum South to continued gross manifestations of white fantasies of themselves as saviors.

In 2018 the response was a bit different as women of color, black women in particular, had let go of white feminist spaces almost entirely. Black and trans women were deeply involved in the online resistance, and calls for reforms of white feminism during and after the 2017 Women's Marches highlighted the lack of inclusion in the growing national movement. The twittersphere came alive with #notmyfeminism and other rejections of feminism in its current reality, namely white and cisgender. One tweet stated "It is SO important that cis feminists say VERY LOUDLY that trans and feminist politics are NOT opposed," and another tweeter responded angrily that "Transgender religiosity is the most conformist, apolitical discourse afloat in decades. The tactics are McCarthyite as well—call outs to all who dare not to conform—especially females." Another response to this exchange offered, "Nay, she's right. Equality for women means black women too. White women alone doesn't cut it. #notmyfeminism."

And so it goes. . . . Fraught with the gaps and missteps that feminism in its multiple iterations has always born, the newest threat to this gender "feminine" oriented intellectual and activist space is, at a minimum, intersectionality if not outright racism, transphobia and the longstanding issues of classism. The mighty battle cry was waged in the words of Flavia Dzodan's now infamous quote, "My feminism will be intersectional or it will be bullshit."[2] We agree with Dzodan and offer that we need to define the bullshit. As our "women" all over the country donned "pussy hats" and attended "women's marches" that January, it became clear that participation meant ignoring the gross exceptionalism and/or essentialism that underpinned this and previous "women's rights" movements. The lack of white identified women and social justice allies at the March for Black Women are part of a consistent pattern of very narrowly focused attentions and allyships coming out of the white feminist space.

In order to don the quintessential pink pussy hat one was required to leave all but their "womanness" at the door. Many of us were not certain whether this iteration of "womanness," which largely excluded women of color unless they left their color at the door, and poor women who could not take off work, find day care, or travel to these marches, and women who were afraid of public exposure, safety, deportation and grossly ignored trans women and non-binary women, was calling us to the table at all. This has been a robust discussion for some time, yet we are not necessarily any closer to creating the antiracist, multiplicitious, trans welcoming, different ability accommodating, queer-led, anti-imperialist, decolonial political movement with numbers in the millions so desperately needed now.

One thing seems increasingly clear, when the pussy hats come out, one's allyship gets violently, if not irreparably, displaced. The tensions between White Feminists and cisgender women and the Movement for Black Lives and Black Lives Matter Global Network seem insurmountable. When the pussy hats were pulled out, this "women's movement" turned their back on the vibrant and courageous activism of Black Lives Matters. One might consider the possibilities had this been a Women's *and* Black Lives Matter March, or simply if it was to have been "a march for all women," it might have simply been a social justice march. Within this tension (including the regular defense of the organizing failures, online violence and debasing exchanges, and the ensuing divisions of a population that would be much stronger when advocating together), white feminists regularly relied on their allyship as a ready defense. This ability to point to their position of protection and savior roles around Black women became a position that had been abandoned in all ways, except for its title. Even originary intents had been lost.

White Feminists and cisgender Women's Studies advocates can do more than "engage" the Movement for Black Lives as allies; they can locate themselves as co-conspirators. Co-conspiracy is a space of shared consequences and a willing loss of social, financial and human capital alongside white cisgender privilege. Allyship is not an identity—it cannot be invoked. Unlike identity, allyship doesn't have its own set of lived experiences and cultures that shape it in a particular way that allows it to be autonomous from other identities. In fact, allyship might have been exactly the opposite had it survived the era of the pussy hat.

The structure of allyship in relationship to the ally-subject, assuming the best of intentions and very hard work on the part of the ally, is fragile and must be continuously performed. Allyship is a one-sided contract that can be undone, underperformed, rescinded, and inauthentically branded in many ways. The greatest failing of allyship is the ability of the ally to enter into this one-sided relationship without the consent of the ally-subject or for that matter having any real connection or contact to the ally-subject. It is important, as we imagine what comes after allyship and other solidaritous spaces that have fallen apart under the failings of white feminism, to really be thoughtful about what would constitute an ally for a new subject position to emerge. Do we accept allies who are bystanders? If not, how do we verify a more active and physical role from someone in that role? What are the degrees to which one might be expected to interact or intervene, for instance?

We do believe that good has occurred under the banner of allyship—from whites involved in anti-racism work to masculine -identifying folk supporting women, femmes, and non-binary persons. However, the standard for allyship is so variable that one can be an ally simply by liking something on Facebook all the way to an ally losing their life at a protest rally, as did Heather Heyer in Charlottesville, VA, on August 12, 2017. We have folks naming themselves "allies" who contribute to the oppression of those they claim allyship to in the regular course of their lives. We have allies who shut down or become violent when they receive feedback that suggests their behaviors in that capacity are not helpful or are outright harmful. We challenge allyship as unsustainable and privileged in that it allows the performer of said allyship to simply stop doing it at the slightest, or with great, provocation. As women of color and trans women share their stories of what they frame as "betrayal" by allies, it becomes painfully clear that there is not a socially just relationship between ally and ally-subject. If one can rescind their allyship because they have been implicated in some harm or misstep, how do we then trust that allyship will stand up as threats to the ally increase—like loss of capital, incarceration or death?

Again, we are not suggesting that good work is not done by so-called allies; it certainly can and has been done. However, if allyship cannot be co-conspiratorial, then allyship simply cannot BE—we need to move beyond the privileged practice of self-naming which is closely related in this space to self-reward and validation. We need to move to a space where social justice folks are focused on doing deep work of solidarity and communal change with all participants expecting and willing to take on necessary levels of consequence. When Tina Fey suggested in her 2017 *Saturday Night Live* skit on the white supremacist rally in Charlottesville, VA, that people eat cake instead of actively responding and protesting, she models the ultimate failure of allyship in her refusal to speak at all. As Susana Morris points out in "For Whites who consider being allies but find it much too tuff," we should "never forget that being a white ally means being less concerned with being called a racist and more concerned with actually perpetuating racism."[3]

We offer allyship as a boundary like all of the boundaries we understand to create and maintain oppression. This parceling or territorializing of identity and position in the white feminist space in particular has kept non-white, non-gender binary participants subjects who are susceptible to the vacillating will of a two-faced ruler. How do we move away from allyship invoked as a talisman or shield of invisible protection around spaces of privilege and hegemony? We understand this as the work of creating coalitional spaces of solidarity: it is language work, thought work, research work, communication work, infrastructural work, legal, social and cultural work. Most importantly, it is unshrinking engagement work where co-conspirators show up without the thought of, or acceptance of, rewards. Getting those in the white cisgender feminist space to receive feedback and move through their own implication is the only way to either save feminism or put it to rest, moving us into another framework that takes up the important issues of gender equity without the deep pitfalls we have been outlining here. These pitfalls remain invisible to many white feminists now pointing to a different crisis in feminism—its engagement in self-help, its preservation of genitalia-based feminism, complaints about its engagements with celebrities, or its soft, commercial character—and this has foreclosed on conversations necessary for coalition building.

Some forty years after the Combahee River Collective offered their engaged deconstruction of feminism, offering that while "eliminating racism in the white women's movement is by definition work for white women to do—work which they would nonetheless continue to demand accountability on," black and brown women, transgender and genderqueer women, and their co-conspirators continue to advance challenges to the status quo of feminist politics.[4] Intersectionality pushes feminist scholars to ask what has been left out of the stories we tell, which experiences are valued, and what types of solutions exist to the continuing problems faced by marginalized groups locally and globally. To that end, it is imperative that we also look at the practices that we believe are helpful, supportive and worth saving in relationship to our non-white, non-binary sisters. It is time to interrogate whether allyship works. More often than not, it actually perpetuates the oppressions that our feminisms seek to disrupt.

NOTES

1. Thirty-nine instances from 2018 when someone called the police to complain about black people doing everyday activities are documented in Niecy Nash's article, "To the Next 'BBQ Becky': Don't Call 911. Call 1-844-WYT-FEAR," *The New York Times* (October 22, 2018), https://www.nytimes.com/2018/10/22/opinion/calling-police-racism-wyt-fear.html, accessed November 10, 2018.

2. Flavia Dzohan, "My Feminism Will Be Intersectional or It Will Be Bullshit," *Tiger Beatdown*, http://tigerbeatdown.com/2011/10/10/my-feminism-will-be-intersectional-or-it-will-be-bullshit/, accessed June 8, 2018.

3. Susana Morris, "For Whites Who Consider Being Allies But Find It Much Too Tuff," in *The Crunk Feminist Collection*, eds. Cooper, Morris and Boylorn. (New York: The Feminist Press at CUNY, 2017): 73.

4. The Combahee River Collective, *The Combahee River Collective Statement: Black Feminist Organizing in the Seventies and Eighties* (Albany, NY: Kitchen Table: Women of Color Press, 1986) reprinted in Manning Marable and Leith Mullings, eds., *Let Nobody Turn Us Around: Voices of Resistance, Reform, and Renewal* (Lanham, MD: Rowman & Littlefield Publishers, Inc., 2000): 525.

INDEX

ABOUT THE EDITORS

Noelle Chaddock is vice president of equity and inclusion at Bates College, where they work with colleagues to cultivate a welcoming, inclusive, equitable and accessible campus community where faculty, staff, students, alumni, community members and future constituents thrive and feel reflected and represented at Bates College. Chaddock oversees the Office of Equity and Inclusion and supports the Office of Intercultural Education as well as working with senior leadership to meet the equity, inclusion, diversity, and accessibility goals of all areas of the college. Chaddock was previously at Rhodes College in Memphis, Tennessee, as an associate provost, and the State University of New York at Cortland where she was the inaugural Chief Diversity Officer. Chaddock earned a PhD in philosophy from Binghamton University. Her scholarly examinations include the spring 2018 original theatre-activism production *Harlem to Hamilton*, a creative collaboration with student directors grounded in pedagogies of teaching black theatre arts to white students at pervasively white institutions and the problematizing of the historical white consumption of black bodies in performance. Chaddock has also recently published articles that look at the role of faculty governance and academic affairs in the work of diversity, equity, and inclusion. She is currently writing and discoursing about genealogical inheritance and disruption, and African American female-identified administrators in higher education critical response roles. Chaddock is a transracial adoptee raised in Endicott, New York, and lives in Maine with her daughter, Morgan Celeste. Chaddock also is privileged to be the mother of Matthew and Joshua Stanley of Endicott.

Beth Hinderliter is assistant professor of art history and director of the Duke Hall Gallery of Fine Art Professor at James Madison University in Virginia, where she works at the intersections of contemporary art history, feminist analysis, and critical race studies. She is interested in the overlapping of art, aesthetics, and politics and how art resists structural oppression and damage-centered narratives. Her recent work in curation includes the exhibition "Colonial Wounds / Postcolonial Repair," which explored colonial violence, memory and reconciliation. She is co-editor of a book on emotion and affect in the Black Lives Matter movement (forthcoming). *More Than Our Pain: Affect and Emotion in the Black Lives Matter Movement* offers historical, analytical and performative studies of the Black Lives Matter movement, revealing how affective and emotive strategies inform and inspire social and political activism in the Black American community. Her previous co-edited volume, *Communities of Sense: Rethinking Aesthetics and Politics* (2008), rethinks the role of our senses in shaping our experiences of community, communal sharing, and politics. Her essays appear in *NKA*, *Journal of Postcolonial Writing*, *TDR*, *African and Black Diaspora*, and *October*.

ABOUT THE CONTRIBUTORS

Laneshia R. Conner, PhD, MSW, CSW is assistant professor in the School of Social Work at Spalding University in Louisville, KY. As a practitioner, she has work experience in child welfare as well as geriatric case management, serving both communities over a span of fifteen years. As an academician, since 2014, she has authored several publications in the fields related to HIV prevention and stigma-reduction among older adults. She has also published and focuses scholarship around adult learning principles, operationalizing best practices for the diverse needs of adult learners in higher education.

Piya Chatterjee is Backstrand Chair and professor of feminist, gender, and sexuality studies at Scripps College. She is the author of *A Time for Tea: Women Labor and Post/Colonial Politics on an Indian Plantation* (2011); co-editor (with Manali Desai and Parama Roy) of *States of Trauma: Gender and Violence in South Asia* (2010); and co-editor (with Sunaina Maira) of *The Imperial University: Academic Repression and Scholarly Dissent* (2014). She is also the editor of a series *Decolonizing Feminisms*. She has served on the National Collective of INCITE: Women of Color against Violence. She lives bi-nationally and has co-organized with rural and plantation women in both tea plantations and southern Bengal, India, for 15 years.

Dr. Vanessa Drew-Branch is assistant professor at Elon University and the owner of VLDrew Consuling Inc. Dr. Drew-Branch received a Bachelor of Science in social work and a Bachelor of Arts in psychology from the California University of Pennsylvania in 2005. She received her EdD in higher education administation, an MSW, and a certificate in public health with a specialty in women's health issues from West Virginia University. Dr. Drew-Branch's academic scholarship focuses on advocacy and social justice through empowering marginalized communities. Her teaching areas include mental health assessment, advocacy practice, human diversity, and social work practice skills. She has expanded her research and practice to include maternal mental health, grief, and loss. Dr. Drew-Branch is a sacred passage end of life doula.

Timothy W. Gerken is associate professor of humanities at the State University of New York Morrisville, where he teaches writing. Gerken served on the SUNY University Faculty Senate's Communittee for Equity, Inclusion, and Diversity, and chaired that committee for the previous three years. In 2017 Gerken was the inaugural recipient of the SUNY Office of Diversity, Equity and Inclusion Award for Diversity, Inclusion, and Social Justice.

Beverly Guy-Sheftall is the founding director of the Women's Research and Resource Center (1981) and the Anna Julia Cooper Professor of women's studies at Spelman College. For many years she was a visiting professor at Emory University's Institute for Women's Studies where she taught graduate courses in women's studies. She has published a number of texts within African-American and women's studies, which have been noted as seminal works by other scholars. She is the past president of the National Women's Studies Association (NWSA) and was recently elected to the National Academy of Arts and Sciences (2017).

Sonyia Richardson is the undergraduate program director and clinical assistant professor in the School of Social Work at the University of North Carolina at Charlotte. She possesses a master degree in social work (University of North Carolina, Chapel Hill) and a bachelor of arts in psychology (University of North Caroline, Charlotte). Additionally, she is a PhD candidate in the curriculum and instruction, urban education specialization (Univesrity of North Carolina, Charlotte). Her research addresses the intersection of social work and urban education. She focuses on providing solutions for systemic education issues, particularly impacting the experiences of Black women.

Magalí Pérez Riedel holds a PhD in communication. Riedel is the author of *Género y Diversidad Sexual en el Blog Boquitas Pintadas* (Gender and Sexual Diversity in the Blog Boquitas Pintadas) and the editor of *Trans Representation on TV and Film* (forthcoming).

Sara Salem is assistant professor in sociology at the London School of Economics. Salem's research interests include political sociology, postcolonial studies, Marxist theory, feminist theory, and global histories of empire and imperialism. She is particularly interested in questions of traveling theory, postcolonial/anti-colonial nationalism, and feminist theory. She has recently published articles on Angela Davis in Egupt in the journal *Signs*; on Frantz Fanon and Egypt's postcolonial state in *Interventions: A Journal of Postcolonial Studies*; and on intersectionality as a travelling theory in the *European Journal of Women's Studies*; among others.

Pablo Scharagrodsky is lecturer and researcher in the Universidad Nacional de Quilmes, Argentina, and Universidad Nacional de La Plata, Argentina. His main area of expertise is the history of education and gender studies.